Red Wine

QUADRILLE

The knowledge.

Red Wine | Peter Grogan

For Ben and Joe

Publishing consultant Jane O'Shea
Editor Simon Davis
Creative director Helen Lewis
Art direction & design Claire Peters
Design Emily Lapworth
Illustrator Claire Peters
Production Vincent Smith, Tom Moore

First published in 2015 by
Quadrille Publishing Limited
www.quadrille.co.uk

Quadrille is an imprint of Hardie Grant.
www.hardiegrant.com.au

Cataloguing in Publication Data:
a catalogue record for this book
is available from the British Library.

ISBN 978 184949 624 7

Printed in the UK

INTRODUCTION

In an auction at Christie's Hong-Kong in November 2013 a dozen bottles of red wine fetched just under half-a-million US dollars. It may only be fermented grape juice, but nothing else we eat or drink attracts anything like the same passion, poetry and pride (as well as price) as red wine.

It's a moderately alcoholic beverage, the typical, drinkable bottle of which costs about half-an-hour's average net pay. To have a chance of understanding why some people will spend the price of one hundred of those bottles on a single sip from one of the most jealously sought-after, we'd better start at square one.

Why is red wine red? It seems like a given that red wine should be made from black grapes and white wine from white grapes – until you consider that most Champagne is made from black grapes. It's the pigments in their skins that provide the colour but they don't have to come into play unless the winemaker wants them to and leaves them to macerate in the juice of the crushed grapes. If the juice and the skins are separated after just a few hours the result will be rosé, and the longer they're left, the darker the wine will be. At the far end of the scale, a bunch of partying Portuguese people 'treading' grapes in a huge stone trough (called a *lagar*) will grind all those pigments into the juice and the result will be something inky-dark that'll end up as Port.

It is in no sense the case, however, that redder means better. Where on the red part of the spectrum the wine in your glass sits also depends on the grape variety and the place where it's grown. As with all spectra, the lines are blurred and the lightest, pinkest reds (made from thin-skinned grapes like Pinot Noir, Gamay and Grenache, for example) are paler than the darkest rosés. But that doesn't imply that they will lack power or depth of flavour. The style of a wine is the other major factor, to the extent that some of the 'biggest' whites – made like reds, with long maceration and ageing in oak casks – can occasionally be mistaken for them in blindfold tastings. They just 'look' white.

Wine of any colour is not just about grapes and places but about the winemakers who take those decisions about style. The best wine is made by people – preferably those who (at some level or other) can call themselves farmers – and not by the machines of agribusiness. Our average bottle of wine may be a drop from the ocean produced across hundreds of square miles of irrigated south-east Australian desert, where the grapes are grown, to all intents and purposes, hydroponically. It won't be unpleasant and it may represent very good, loss-leading value, but for wine with more character and complexity there is no doubt that smaller is better and smallest is best.

Those forty-thousand-dollar bottles came from a Burgundy vineyard a couple of hundred metres square that is owned by some very rich 'farmers' but the principle is still the same – the wine we want is something that somebody is proud to put their name on. Cloth-capped Cockneys used to borrow the word claret as slang for blood, and it's true that while white wines appeal first to the head, reds speak to the heart – and when they do, the talk is all about essence and intensity and life force.

1 MAKING RED WINE

WINEMAKING CAN BE SIMPLE. IN SOUTH LONDON, THE Urban Wine Company solicits contributions of random grapes from people's gardens to make into Château Tooting – the 'grey goo' of wine. It can also be complex, such that budding winemakers the world over, having done their ten- or 15-year apprenticeship in a few cutting-edge wineries dotted about the globe, will set out to find a vineyard of their own and their shopping-list will be something like this (stick with me – you've got to earn that first glass)...

They will know what sort of plot they want in terms of the soil type, the latitude, the altitude, the aspect, the slope, the hours of sunshine and the amount of rainfall it will get (or the amount of irrigation it will need). These factors will be related to the preferred conditions for the varieties of grapes they want to plant.

They will have plans for the density of planting of those vines, the control of the yield per acre through early pruning of bunches and for canopy management, i.e. cutting back the leaves to let the grapes feel enough of the sun. They will have plans for organic and maybe biodynamic methods of fertilization and pest control and they will expect to obsessively check ripeness in terms of must weight and the pH of the juice as they near the harvest.

The picking and sorting of the grapes will be done by hand, the 'crush' will be carefully controlled (not too much – it's not fruit juice!), as will the temperature and duration of the maceration and fermentation and the choice of vessels in which they each take place. The induction (or prevention) of a secondary fermentation; the choice of oak or other materials and the presence or absence of the lees during ageing and the length of that process will have exercised them greatly and any blending of different batches to assemble the final wine will keep them busy.

They will have known from day one what the characteristics – the *style* – of the wine they are going to make will be and that it will be good, but the real, secret beauty of wine is that even they won't – *can't* – know exactly what it will taste like. Except that it won't taste like Château Tooting – and to find out why that's the case, we need to go back to the basics .

GRAPES

'The wine she drinks is made of grapes,' said the Bard, and it's a good idea to keep it that way. But it's not just made from any old grapes; it's specifically the several thousand or so varieties of *vitis vinifera* – the clue is in the name. The rest are table grapes destined for the fruitbowl or for drying into sultanas and what-have-you.

Grapevines are admirable things and unfussy, to say the least. In fact, they thrive – and produce their finest fruits – in adversity, planted in poor soils in climates where they will struggle to achieve full ripeness. Regardless of variety, old vines make better wines than young ones; their deep root systems are their insurance policy against drought and they also suck up a wider variety of nutrients, which ultimately results in a more complex range of flavours.

Grapevines can live for several hundred years, although most have a productive life about as long as a human one. There are further parallels and I know I'd rather get to grips with a 40-year-old of an unfashionable variety that knows its way around the block than mess around with a callow youth of the most on-trend variety – they don't know they're born. Vines have no insurance against the weather and achieving ripeness is more of a crapshoot in any given place in any given vintage. One thing is for sure, though – good wine was never made from unripe grapes.

The variety of the vine is the biggest single influence on just how 'red' a red wine is. Thin-skinned grapes, like Pinot Noir, Gamay and Grenache have less pigment and naturally produce lighter-coloured wines, while others – Syrah, Malbec and Zinfandel spring to mind – are predisposed to produce fuller, darker ones.

TERROIR

In the traditional winemaking regions of Europe, things presumably started out fairly randomly – people made wine out of whatever was to hand – and only evolved through long experiment into growing the grape best suited to the local conditions. The soil of the slopes along some of the great wine rivers – the Rhône, the Rhine and the Douro, to name a few – must be so suffused with the stuff of countless generations of vines that have thrived and then fallen along them since pre-Roman times that it is its very essence, its DNA. Not literally, maybe, but that's the sort of thing people rhapsodize about when they talk about the concept of '*terroir*'. I do wish sometimes they'd put a cork in it.

Terroir does have meaning but it seems to be explicable by mundane meteorology and geography and – crucially – it increasingly appears therefore to be replicable. If *terroir* means the influence of the place in which a grapevine is grown; specifically the type of soil, the weather and the exposure of the vines to it in terms of altitude and aspect – then there can be no holy sites.

It's precisely this that pioneering winemakers the world over are betting on as they scour the earth looking for the best sites in places where land is cheap. And it is also as a direct result of this kind of disruptive innovation that it's possible the world of wine – in terms of who grows what, and where – may have changed more in the last 20 years than in the previous 2000. When a top winemaker told me, 'It's a full-time job just keeping up with everything that's happening,' he seemed as much exasperated as exhilarated.

WHAT'S IN A PLACE?

Terroir-deniers, by the way, need only to splash out on a few wines from a handful of the different crus (vineyards) of a Burgundy village – Grèves, Clos des Mouches and Clos du Roi in Beaune, for example, preferably made by the same winemaker – to see the light. It's a serious eye-opener to discover just how multifarious the wines made from a single grape variety can be when grown in different situations, albeit sometimes only a stone's throw apart.

THE ROLE OF THE WINEMAKER – IN THE VINEYARD

If grape varieties and the places in which they are grown provide the characters and the scene for the story of a wine, it's what the winemaker chooses to do with them – both in the vineyard and in the winery – that provides the plot.

It's not a coincidence that most great wines are made from blends of grape varieties. This is not to say that some single grapes can't make complex wines – a great Burgundy or Hermitage (see pages 32 and 44) proves the point as well as a great one-handed pianist proves his. But most grapes need a bit of help here and there to get the balance right and it's good that more and more southern hemisphere winemakers are coming round to this. A choice of different varieties in the vineyard gives them complexity on tap but it's up to them to keep it subtle.

Winemakers' decisions about the ripeness of the grapes are weighty matters, and choosing exactly when to pick the grapes is the biggest question for most producers. Earlier harvesting makes for lighter, leaner wines with higher levels of acidity. The later they leave it, the richer and denser the result, and higher levels of sugar (and, eventually, alcohol) are the cause. Acidity is the life force, the electricity of wine and is especially important when it comes to lighter reds – it's one half of a balancing act with the sweetness of the fruit sugars, and without it wine is just fruit juice with vodka: an alcopop.

Many of the world's most acclaimed wines at all but the lowest price levels are now produced organically and even biodynamically – a sort of agricultural homeopathy, some of the tenets of which, if it weren't for the results, would stretch credulity to near breaking point. It is frankly a matter of disinterest to me if biodynamic winemakers are putting a bit of powdered cow-horn into the fertilizer or burying a sheep's head at dawn in a corner of the vineyard on a 'flower day' or a 'root day' or any other day, but what shines through most of the time is their commitment to quality. Most of these people would make great wine on the moon if push came to shove, so let's just let them get on with it because the wines are often spectacular.

There is, for sure, more in the heaven and earth of winemaking than is dreamt of in most of our philosophies. Everything affects wine, even the weather at the point of consumption: temperature, humidity and atmospheric pressure and many mysteries remain to be worked out. A Californian winemaker once said to me; 'Let's try the Pinot Noir first – it really likes sunny days,' and she wasn't joking.

Alone on planet organic, winemakers often don't advertise their green credentials. They know that a healthy soil full of manure (and horses are making a comeback in the vineyard) makes for healthier grapes than one full of chemical fertilizers and pesticides but they have no need of bandwagons when it comes to selling their wines.

THE ROLE OF THE WINEMAKER – IN THE WINERY

Once they're gathered in (and hopefully sorted to remove any dodgy or rotten ones and de-stemmed because stalks don't taste any better in your wine than if you eat one) it's time for what's called 'the crush' – the first transformative step in the metamorphosis from grape to wine. Like all the other steps it's important and – regardless of whether it's carried out by picturesque peasants treading the grapes in a deep stone trough called a *lagar*, as they still sometimes do in northern Portugal, or by a great industrial machine – the point is to squeeze every drop of flavour out.

Like most stages of winemaking. the length of time the crushed grapes are left to macerate is a big factor. The more solid matter is released over time, the darker, deeper and – literally – heavier the wine will be. Winemaking is a nerve-racking business and it's another judgement call – if the juice spends too much time on the broken skins, the effect can be overwhelming and there is a risk of extracting too many of the mouth-puckering flavour compounds called tannins.

A leading Aussie winemaker once told me apropos of his own top grapes-on-steroids bottlings: 'No worries, mate. They're not for drinking, they're for winning prizes.' Thankfully this tendency for over-extracting and using super-ripe grapes for showing-off purposes is on the wane. It seems to have taken an awfully long time to work out that – with wine as with most other things in life – bigger is not necessarily better, and balance is everything.

NAPA VALLEY BORDEAUX BLENDS – *CALIFORNIA DREAMIN'*

'Meritage' is a ghastly word (that's supposed to rhyme with 'heritage') and it means a Bordeaux-style blend of grape varieties and is most often used in California, particularly the Napa Valley, where they have always ploughed their own furrow. They don't care what the rest of the world thinks about their increasingly anachronistic, over-extracted fruit bombs and they sure as hell don't need our money.

This is a shame, because when most people think about Californian wine the only experience they have is of the cheap, mass-produced stuff from the Central Valley. Comparatively little of the high-end wine is exported and – love 'em or loathe 'em – there's no denying that there is quality there in spades. The flavours are pure, primary fruit – blackcurrants abound – the more-is-more approach that most wine regions are gradually maturing away from. This sort of wine is the stadium-rock, electric guitar solo to the finger-picking acoustic; there is room for both on my MP3 player and if intensity is what you prize above all then Napa does it better than anywhere (and prices at the very top reflect this with sticker-shocking clarity).

The fermentation process – which involves the digestion of the carbohydrates (i.e. the fruit sugars) by yeasts that turn them into carbon dioxide and ethanol (i.e. alcohol) – is what turns the juice into wine. Like most stages of winemaking, longer is better but quicker is cheaper, so it can be a fast and foamy industrial process taking place over a few days or a mysterious, slow, unstable one done over several months at low temperatures using wild airborne yeasts to make newfangled, so-called 'natural wines'.

The amount of alcohol that results from the process is variable (but nothing like as variable as it is for white wines) and depends on the amount of sugar in the grapes (which in turn depends on their ripeness). It ranges from around 11–16 per cent and is controllable to an extent by the winemaker. It is one of the major factors – along with the amount of solid matter – that gives a wine body. Alcohol levels are, thankfully, gradually coming down.

To filter or not to filter is the next dilemma. Unfiltered wines are usually better because the wine can continue to develop in the bottle, but there is the problem of pesky sediment. As with a lot of badly kept or badly served craft beers the phrase 'It's supposed to be cloudy' should be consumed with a pinch of salt.

The French use the terms *assemblage* and *élevage* for what happens next in the winery. The first means putting the bulk of the wine together to get the basic style the winemaker wants. This is done by blending batches made either from different grapes or from the same grapes but grown in different parts of the vineyard or village or region, or both.

Élevage – whether called something industrial-sounding that happens in a factory full of white-coated technicians or done by a man in a beret scurrying around in a dank cellar – is the arcane work of getting the best result from all the wine that is at hand. It means 'raising up' and it's about distributing some of the brighter and fresher (or indeed deeper and richer) wine among the ho-hums to raise the quality of the whole lot as far as possible (while still keeping some of the best stuff to sell for more money, of course).

A corporate winemaker may perhaps be looking for the least-worst result while the man in the beret is looking for the best possible but they are probably both nice people. As Abe Lincoln said of habitual drunkards (a group from whom they are not always entirely indistinguishable) – 'Their heads and hearts will bear an advantageous comparison with those of any other class.' Whatever they do, it's alchemy as far as I'm concerned.

AGEING

Once all the blending and balancing acts have been done, it's time for the long silence. Age is the fourth dimension of wine and its importance cannot be overestimated. Time softens the tannins within the wine from cold, black tea into melty, vanilla tones and lets the pesky 'primary' fruit flavours evolve into rich, complex, almost endlessly nuanced ones – things like the cedar cigar box, leather, tobacco, coffee and violets that people like me bang on about.

ONE TO DRINK

CHÂTEAUNEUF-DU-PAPE – THE POPE KNOWS

With 13 different grape varieties permitted in its production, Châteauneuf, which became France's first demarcated wine region in 1923, is the daddy of blended wines. Very few vignerons take up the whole offer – most stick to a handful – but it's no big surprise that this free hand should result in a huge diversity of styles and wines that can be either light, medium or full-bodied.

No surprise either that the wines should be complex, but they all have something in common which is often characterized as a certain rusticity, a farmyardiness – usually in a nice way – and aromas that are often likened to the smell of *garrigue*: the low-growing, bushy plants like juniper, broom and wild rosemary and thyme of the southern French uplands.

The fruit is usually black and brambly, and with the immeasurable benefit of a few years of age it mulches down into a savoury, spicy soup with the aromas magically morphing into leather and tobacco. All this comes at a price, and sadly the mere presence of the name on a label comes with no guarantees. Nonetheless those 1923 regulations bring with them the happy collateral that many top Châteauneuf producers also make fabulous wines that have to be labelled as Côtes-du-Rhône as some of their vineyard lies beyond the boundaries of the appellation. Seek them out.

This ageing is often done in two stages: in barrel and then in bottle. If the winemaker wants the classic, toasty edge of much high-end red Bordeaux, for example – and the wine has enough quality not to be overwhelmed by it – he'll use expensive 225-litre *barriques* made of new, vanilla-rich oak. For cheaper wines, he will reverse the process and put the barrel into the wine – toasted oak chips are bunged into vast steel or concrete ageing vats to give a whiff of class.

'Peak oak' appears to have been reached some time ago, though, with winemakers in many regions preferring to let the fruit flavours speak (and evolve) for themselves. (They've been doing that for centuries along the Rhône using ancient *foudres* of up to 12,000 litres which impart very little oak influence, so *plus ça change*.) Nonetheless, oak is still crucially important in regions like Bordeaux and Burgundy as well as in California and the southern hemisphere and the basic rule is, again, balance. Lighter, fresher wines need less oak – just a caress, a kiss on the cheek and not a full-on snog with tongues.

Barrel ageing – of whatever type – can run from a matter of weeks to several years and is a fine thing as long as the wine itself has the stuffing to benefit from it. With the same caveat, the development process continues once the wine is bottled (and some European regions set minimum ageing requirements before a wine can be labelled reserva/riserva or the like).

So, in summary, all we're looking for from our winemaker is a light touch, balance, subtlety, complexity and maturity. In a single word, harmony. It's not a lot to ask, is it?

A QUESTION OF TIME?

It's worth pointing out that there is nothing wrong with young wine per se, as long as it's made to be drunk young. Most Beaujolais and Loire reds and lots of the light reds of northern Italy and Germany and cool-climate reds from all corners don't have the tannins to make old bones and I'm all for enjoying their crisp, fruity charms a.s.a.p.

But too young is not OK. It is often the result of corporate penny-pinching in that storage costs money and a just-in-time economy waits for no wine. It's a pipe-dream to hope that more producers will emulate those in Spain and Italy and only release their best wines when they're ready to drink, but you can always take on the job yourself (see page 130).

2 THE MAJOR GRAPE VARIETIES

MY DAD LIKED HIS WINE, ALBEIT ONLY FOR SPECIAL occasions – beer and whisky were for everyday – but I doubt that he knew the names of many (or maybe even any) of the grape varieties that went into making his favourite wines from Bordeaux, Burgundy and, especially, the Rhône. In those days, people navigated the world of wine by the names of places, not of grapes. Today, for better or worse, the vast majority of wine drinkers have their favourite varieties.

For centuries, European colonists naturally enough took their own favoured grape varieties with them to wherever they hoped they might thrive. (The traffic eventually became two-way and in the mid-19th century, when Europe's vineyards were devastated by the *phylloxera* louse, vast quantities of healthy rootstock were re-imported from the Americas to replace the diseased ones.) The game nowadays is global and viral-fast and a Chilean winemaker mulling over the possibilities for an obscure Italian grape variety in a cool-climate Australian vineyard is no biggie.

But before pondering planting an unpronounceable Austrian variety in an even cooler Andean vineyard our budding winemaker needs to earn his spurs with one of the headline grapes. Often called the international varieties, they're some of the ones that the people down the pub are asking for by name.

CABERNET SAUVIGNON

The stage may have been a lot smaller when Cab Sauv grabbed the centre of it in the 1980s but, if your previous credits include playing the lead in the 'first growth' clarets that sell for hundreds - even thousands - of pounds a bottle, then the top of the bill would seem like only your rightful place. Bordeaux is still Cab's box-office but the show now plays across the world, winning rave reviews everywhere.

Cabernet Sauvignon may seem ubiquitous but it's not quite as widespread as it was 20 years ago. It doesn't thrive everywhere, as Kiwi winemakers found out to their initial cost (and later good fortune in replacing it with Pinot Noir). Australia (especially Coonawarra, McLaren Vale and Langhorne Creek) and the USA (Napa Valley, Sonoma, Oregon and Washington) have specialized in the blockbuster, fruit-bomb single-varietal wines that can rival top Bordeaux for price. Thankfully, they are now turning towards more balanced wines, often blended with the usual Bordeaux varieties. Chile (Aconcagua, Colchagua and Maipo valleys) and Argentina (Mendoza, Luján de Cuyo) have been making mini-me versions at micro-me prices for decades. South Africa's Stellenbosch and Paarl regions are now staking a claim to the southern hemisphere's finest cabernets.

The first time most people over 50 saw the words 'Cabernet' and 'Sauvignon' was on bottles of surprisingly slurpable (especially given the price) Bulgarian wines in the 1980s. They seemed to disappear in the '90s for some reason but they're now making a nostalgia-tinted comeback. In the north of Italy Cab Sauv has been playing a discreet (and sometimes illegal) role in blends for 200 years. It's much more brazen in the 'Supertuscan' wines further south. Yes, Cab's almost everywhere.

Blackcurrants – leaves, stems and all – is the descriptive term on everybody's lips but the young wine often gives a clue to Cab's antecedents – a high-pitched, green pepper note that comes from the Sauvignon Blanc side of a random coupling with dark and brooding Cabernet Franc. Ageing in new oak barrels (and then in bottle) makes those flavours bloom into something much more complex and appealing – the summer pudding turns into a rich, mature fruit cake.

So a standing ovation for Cabernet Sauvignon – along with Chardonnay, the first of the superstar grape varieties and very often the first that people get to know by name. It has been over-used and abused but it remains a class act, as a look at any list of the world's finest and most expensive wines proves; it makes more of them than all the rest of the cast put together.

PINOT NOIR

What Cabernet Sauvignon is to Bordeaux, Pinot Noir is to Burgundy, only more so. Apart from some Gamay here and there Pinot is the only grape in town. It comes with a certain amount of baggage, its main fault having been an apparent reluctance to make any decent wine that didn't cost a fortune. But things have changed and after lots of research into different clones it's finally possible to get a glimpse of Pinot glory at an everyday price from north-eastern Italy, Romania – where it is doing encouraging things for the lowest end of the market – Germany (as **Spätburgunder**), Austria (as **Blauburgunder**) and across the southern hemisphere, notably in Australia's Mornington Peninsula and Yarra Valley, and in New Zealand and Chile.

The tweedy merchants used to say of Burgundy 'Drink 'em young and jammy or old and gamey'. Wheresoever your Pinot comes from, the jam will usually be of the strawberry variety, often with a lick of smoky oak around the edges and maybe a touch of coffee. Only time will tell whether the best southern-hemisphere wines will have the legs to get to that glorious, gamey stage where damp, mushroomy underbrush mingles with something animal, like bloody, red meat.

MERLOT

Merlot has had a bit of a rocky time of late, especially for a grape that makes some of France's (and hence the world's) greatest red wines, specifically on Bordeaux's right bank of the Gironde river in Pomerol and St-Émilion. Some of the criticism is justified and it has to an extent been the victim of own success in places like California, Washington State, Australia, New Zealand and Chile.

The problem is that it's not that easy to get it to full ripeness and when it's bad, it's very, very bad – mean and green, thin and tart. But when it's good it can be very, very good with its natural

ONE TO DRINK

CÔTE D'OR PREMIER CRU BURGUNDY – THE GOLD STANDARD

Pinot Noir is the princess of grapes for unplugged wines, Burgundy is its boudoir and the *premier* and *grand cru* wines among its most perfect, perfumed productions. The Côte d'Or typically makes pale wines that are full of scent, seduction and secrets and none more so than those from Chambolle-Musigny, often described as the most 'feminine' of Burgundies. But the lightness doesn't mean they lack depth and intensity – the best have layers of flavour that seem to go on forever.

Raspberries and strawberries are often the starting point for describing them but there's something more ethereal in the good stuff and people often talk about loamy, woodsy things and well-hung game and blood and leather when they get excited. Even if we never get to taste the likes of a fine vintage of a Chambolle-Musigny 1er Cru Les Amoureuses (Oh! such names they have) we should be grateful: forty-odd years ago it was a glass of one such in an Oxford restaurant that first turned the young wine critic Jancis Robinson's head.

plumminess (accentuated by a sprig of mint) harmonizing with age into an opulent Christmas pudding. At its best, Merlot is one of the few red wine grapes that can shine with no help from blending partners. The finest Pomerols have layers of flavour from intense, creamy black fruits through liquorice and spice to something like kirsch and mocha. They ain't cheap.

Merlot is important in blending in the wines of Bordeaux's left bank and has spread throughout Europe as well as the southern hemisphere. It can make crisp, light, fresh wines at altitude in northern Italy (Friuli, Trentino-Alto Adige) – and even great 'Supertuscans' further south (see page 66). In Italian Switzerland, in Ticino, it is often a monoculture, furnishing the whites, rosés and fizz as well as the reds. It was confused with Carmenère in South America for ages (although I've never been convinced that they weren't simply trying to disown it).

TEMPRANILLO

Tempranillo is Spain's answer to Cabernet Sauvignon – very widespread, highly versatile and best when blended to make the finest, age-worthy wines of both Rioja and Ribera del Duero. And like Cab Sauv, it's a bit of a chameleon. Pinning it down in terms of primary tastes and aromas is difficult and its biggest assets are its depth of colour, silkiness of texture and natural affinity for ageing in oak. So the words people reach for are the ones that reflect what the winemaker turns the fruit flavours into – lots of things like caramel and chocolate and leather and tobacco and spice.

It's the most widely planted grape in Spain, under a bunch of different names: **Ull de Llebre** ('hare's eye') in Catalonia, **Cencibel** in Valdepeñas and **Tinta de Toro** in Toro – where it makes particularly intense, bull-in-a-china-shop wines – and it's now spreading with some success into California, Argentina and Australia.

NEBBIOLO

Nebbiolo is the Barolo and Barbaresco grape of Italy's north-western Piedmont region. It's possible to be that specific because – unusually for a big-name grape these days – it is almost entirely confined to that one area. OK, it sneaks out into the rest of Piedmont a bit (Langhe, Carema, Gattinara), sometimes under the aliases of **Spanna** or **Chiavennasca** (in Lombardy) and puts in the odd cameo appearance in California, Washington State and Australia (King Valley) but that really is about it.

Pinot Noir, the grape with which Nebbiolo is most often compared, has a reputation of being difficult but it is one of the lads, happy to doss on the floor, compared to his nebs. This is often the case where the genes are unstable (look at royal families the world over) and Nebbiolo exists in a number of clonal varieties (as is the case with Pinot Noir).

ONE TO DRINK

BAROLO – DON'T DISCOUNT IT (ESPECIALLY IF SOMEBODY ELSE DOES)

Made from the Nebbiolo grape in a five-mile-square postage stamp in north-western Italy's Piemonte region, I reckon that Barolo – of all the great red wines of the world – is the one that the least number of people have tasted. That's a shame because when it's good it's unlike anything else, but the situation is gradually changing. The reason is that economic conditions in Italy seem to be making it harder for the excellent local co-operative producers to sell their wines at the prices that they're used to getting and, rather than risk lowering the price in the domestic market, they've been shipping it off to northern Europe, notably to the discount supermarket chains.

A few years ago it was either impossible or unwise to buy any Barolo for as little as two or three times the cost of the average bottle of wine but no longer. So if your first look at its often very pale exterior, tinged with a bricky edge after only a few years of age, draws you in, you'll find dried roses and leather mixing with a haunting, bonfire smokiness in the aromas and rich Turkish delight and coffee in the flavours. It's impossible to resist a comparison with Burgundy – including prices at the top end – and any Pinot Noir fanciers are seriously missing out if they don't head for their nearest discounter.

Apart from that it will only thrive on south- and south-west-facing slopes (preferably of calcareous marl or sandy soil) at an altitude of between 750 and 1500 feet. And it likes its newspaper to be carefully ironed each morning. The Pinot parallels extend to the wine itself – pale, ethereal, woodsy and famously perfumed with tar and roses. When it's good, there's nothing quite like it. And when it's bad it's atrocious.

SANGIOVESE

Like many Italian grapes, Sangiovese has a lot of names – **Sangiovete**, **Brunello** and **Morellino** among them – and a limited appetite for travel. Mind you, if I ruled the roost in Tuscany, I dare say I'd be the same. The fact that it's the Chianti grape might – at least until recently – put some people off, but in the best of those wines, and in Brunello di Montalcino and Vino Nobile di Montepulciano, it produces some of Italy's greatest wines.

There are always cherries – red and tartly fresh in straightforward, young wines; the black morello type in more ambitious ones and richly, spicily stewed with bitter chocolate and leather in the best. And there are always almonds – with a puckering bitter edge at one end of the scale and a mellow toastiness at the other.

Sangiovese is the most widely planted grape variety in Italy and the mainstay of the central regions, where good value can be found on Tuscany's coast (Morellino di Scansano, Maremma) as well as in Umbria, Emilia-Romagna and Le Marche (Rosso Piceno). It's blended with Montepulciano in the south-east, has made headway in Corsica (as **Nielluccio**) and is taking tentative steps in Argentina, home to many Italian migrants.

SYRAH/SHIRAZ

One grape, known by two names, that's grown in every major wine-producing country in the world and makes wines with flavours that range from blackberries to black olives? We'd better start at the beginning...

The notion that it originated in Shiraz, Persia, seems to have been debunked, and France's Rhône Valley – where it's called Syrah – is thought to be the cradle, especially the northern part, where it's the only black grape used to make the region's spicy, heart-warming reds. The catch is – there's *always* a catch – you'll never see that name on a label (it's an *appellation controlée* thing).

Where you will see the name is on labels of wines from elsewhere in France – IGP Pays d'Oc, for example – *but* (and you may need a big sip at this point) producers often use the grape's other name, Shiraz, because that's the name we're used to seeing on bottles of our favourite rambunctious Aussie reds (especially from the Barossa Valley, see page 110).

Those wines took the world by storm in the early '90s and the rest of the world soon started to get in on the action. 'The

ONE TO DRINK

CHIANTI CLASSICO – NO MORE FIASCOS

The name has been abused for decades, all the rules have been broken, re-made and broken again and many a tart, thin wine has left the region in the raffia-covered bottle called, appropriately enough, a *fiasco*, but Chianti can still make great wine. Always made principally from Sangiovese and always with the bitter almonds and puckering little red cherries that seem essential to so many Italian wines, regardless of what they're made of (just why *is* that?), finding a good Chianti is always worth the effort.

Most likely it will be from the central 'Classico' part of what is far too big a region for its own good – the fact that it was one of the earliest demarcated wine regions (1716) means that isn't going to change any time soon. While the rank of *riserva* is no absolute guarantee of anything much other than a certain amount of ageing – but is it two years or 34 months? Nobody seems to be certain even of that but, hey: it's Italy, and it still narrows the odds.

With a few years' more cellar age the primary flavours evolve and those cherries stew down to a chocolatey essence; the aromas turn to dusty, autumnal tones of dry leaves and herbs, and as the Medici *marchese* and his retinue clatter into the courtyard after a day in pursuit of *cinghiale*, the feasting tables are laid...

bigger the better' seemed to be the idea for some of the heavy, wintergreen-scented wines of a few years ago. A move in recent years across the southern hemisphere towards lighter, fresher, more balanced styles – often made from grapes grown at cooler, higher altitudes – has come as a welcome relief.

Everywhere they are made (and they are also made to especially good effect in New Zealand, Chile and South Africa) the wines are always bold, with black-fruit flavours and usually a twist of black pepper. Back at base, as you go further up the Rhône Valley, those flavours evolve into a rich and savoury spice-fest (where those black olives come in) that is the benchmark the world over.

GAMAY

It's the Beaujolais grape. It is grown successfully in other parts of France (notably the Loire and – blended with a minimum one-third of Pinot Noir and mendaciously called **Passe-tout-grains** in Burgundy) but few grapevines are as firmly rooted in one place as Gamay. Sprightly, chillable, swillable rapidly improving light reds stuffed with red-cherry fruitiness are almost always the result. So the best wines from the top Beaujolais *villages* of Moulin-à-Vent and Morgon come as a surprise. They're the Mr Hyde to Gamay's usual Dr Jekyll – dark and dense and brooding (at least by comparison), with deep damsons instead of cherries and well worth ageing for up to ten years.

GRENACHE

Given that it's the second most widely planted grape variety on the planet, Grenache keeps a low profile. The grapes are relatively low in tannins and, unblended, it makes ripe, round wines with a touch of sweetness often described as jammy. It's at its best as a team player, bringing out the best in other grapes. This, and the fact that until very recently the French have disdained to mention grape varieties on their wine labels, are the reasons for the low profile.

Southern Rhône's Châteauneuf-du-Pape (see page 22) region makes rather grand wines in which Grenache reigns supreme among the 13 permitted grape varieties. It's also the cornerstone (as **Garnacha**) in up-and-coming Priorato in north-eastern Spain where, a little further west, it also gets the award for best supporting role in Rioja, providing the fruitiness to soften the darker, denser tones of Tempranillo. Sardinia's finest red wines are a dark and uncharacteristically macho style of Grenache which does business there under the alias of **Canonau**.

ONE TO DRINK

HERMITAGE – HOLY-MOLY

There is a tiny little chapel – the source of the name – near the top of the tumbling granite slopes of Hermitage along the east bank of the northern Rhône which has been a place of homage for winemakers the world over. Not literally, perhaps, but in less litigious times South African and Australian winemakers used to borrow the name for the wines that they were proudest of.

It's not hard to see why. Syrah vines are thought to have been cultivated here since pre-Roman times and the rite of transforming the juice of their fruits into pepper-scented wine seems to be embedded as much in the DNA of the celebrants as it is in the soil that they rise out of.

The young wines have a stunningly intense purity of fruit which even the arch-advocates of the benefits of ageing wine might rue the dimming of were it not for the fact that it transubstantiates into a sacred, savoury essence of herbs and spice and something like black olives and... bacon. 'The wine tastes of bacon?' they scoff. And then they taste it.

WHAT'S IN A NAME

Carignan – A.K.A. *Cariñena, Mazuelo*

Grenache – A.K.A. *Garnacha, Canonau*

Malbec – A.K.A. *Côt, Auxerrois*

Mourvèdre – A.K.A. *Mataro, Monastrell*

Nebbiolo – A.K.A. *Spanna, Chiavennasca*

Pinot Noir – A.K.A. *Spätburgunder, Blauburgunder*

Sangiovese – A.K.A. *Sangiovete, Brunello, Morellino*

Syrah – A.K.A. *Shiraz*

Tempranillo – A.K.A. *Ull de Llebre, Cencibel, Tinta de Toro*

Zinfandel – A.K.A. *Primitivo, Crljenak Kaštelanski*

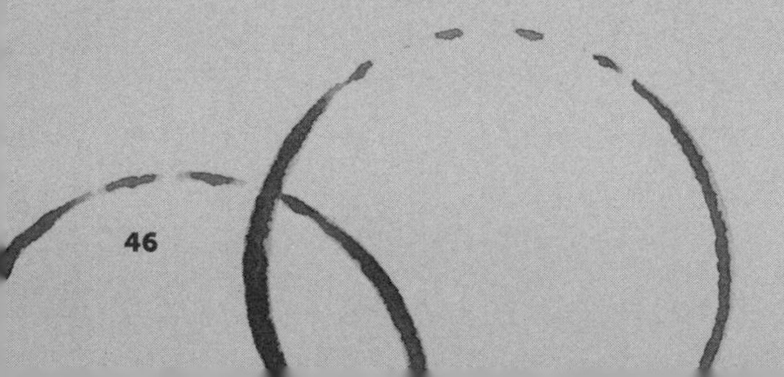

ZINFANDEL

Last but never least (in terms of heft if nothing else), science has discovered that California's Zinfandel is made of the same genetic stuff as the southern Italian **Primitivo** grape. It's also Croatia's **Crljenak Kaštelanski**, but as long as it's making choccy-full wines stuffed with rich blackcurrant and cherry fruit with a whiff of cloves, why worry? Some California versions can be overwhelming and hard to tackle without food but the best are rich and spicy in the Malbec mould.

In the heat of Puglia and Sicily the Italians usually blend it, often to take the edge off the even madder Negroamaro (the clue is in the name, 'black bitter'). Those Croatian wines – and others made from Plavac Mali, a close cousin – can be excellent (and expensive) and are slowly making headway in international markets.

3 OTHER INTERESTING GRAPE VARIETIES

THE GREAT WINE REGIONS SOUTH OF THE EQUATOR AND in California made their names mainly by producing single-varietal wines that could hold a candle to those of the traditional European places. So the Barossa Shiraz cat could look at the northern Rhône king, for example, or that of Californian or Chilean Cabernet at claret.

They've been there and done that now and thankfully there's a lot more blending of grapes going on south of the equator these days. It's almost always a good thing – the medieval monks of Châteauneuf-du-Pape didn't use up to a baker's dozen of different grapes (including three white varieties) just because they *could*. They knew it made for more fascinating wines and it still does.

Some grapes do still seem wedded to a particular place but even the most obdurate Italian (Nebbiolo, Sangiovese) and Spanish (Tempranillo, Graciano) varieties are now under the microscope in California and the southern hemisphere. Thankfully, the picture is very different from how it looked in the '80s and '90s, when it seemed like Cabernet Sauvignon and Merlot were set for a global duopoly.

That must have seemed like a good idea to the big wine corporations, with their desire for uniformity, predictability, and the increase in profit margin that such things bring about, but for the drinker a big part of the pleasure of wine is in its very diversity. So the wheel turns and now all over Europe it is the indigenous grapes that are feeling the love and are now even being replanted in preference over these so-called 'international' varieties.

Some of the following ten varieties are no-brainers for inclusion in a chapter such as this but some just made the cut from a very long list of deserving cases (there's another list of ten in brief at the end because I couldn't bear to leave them out). There could have been 50 and you should know one thing: the list won't be the same in ten years' time.

BARBERA

Barbera is the understudy grape of north-western Italy's Piedmont region, after the Nebbiolo of Barolo and Barbaresco fame (not to mention fortune). Of course, being Italy there are, in fact, loads of other varieties but Barbera is now one of the few widely planted Italian varieties that are also dotted around the world (notably in Argentina, Australia and California and pretty much anywhere where a lot of Italain immigrants settled in the nineteenth and twentieth centuries.).

Barbera is very versatile and makes everything from frilly, sweet *frizzante* through to long-lived, oak-aged wines (especially around Asti and Alba) which, true to their Italian roots, always come with a dollop of cherries and a sprinkle of almonds. I'm a fan, as is one of the top Barolo producers who has to bottle much of his wine under the much lowlier Langhe DOC as he insists on adding some Barbera to his Nebbiolo to beef it up and is prepared to take the consequences.

CABERNET FRANC

When wine writers bang on about 'notes of lead *pencil*' or 'pencil shavings' on the 'nose' of a claret, this is the grape responsible. I would apologize on their behalves but for one thing – there's no more accurate way of describing a particular whiff of graphite that Cab Franc (pron. 'fronk') gives off (especially when ageing in new oak contributes the 'shavings' aspect). In any case, it's easier to deal with than another aroma which can sometimes occur and which I'll euphemize as the 'fecal element'. Yes, it can occasionally smell of poo, and it's either something you can deal with or you can't.

Most often blended in small quantities in Bordeaux (especially on the right bank around St-Émilion), on its own it makes elegant, minerally reds and rosés all along the Loire. It also pops up to good effect in single-varietal wines in north-eastern Italy (Friuli-Venezia Giulia) and California and pretty much everywhere people make Bordeaux blends.

CARIGNAN

Carignan has traditionally been a very widespread grape in southern France and Spain (as **Cariñena** in the north-east and in Rioja as **Mazuelo**). Too productive for its own good in the past, especially among subsistence farmers for whom quantity was the only criterion, it is now rehabilitating itself after a lifetime spent churning out oceans of plonk in the Languedoc and South-West. The best – big and brambly with plenty of acidity – are from Corbières, though Chile and California have caught on too.

CINSAULT

Another unassuming team player among grapes – it's even prepared to sacrifice one of its letters for the common cause and be spelled **Cinsaut** in France – this grape makes herb-filled, sinewy wines often blended with one or more (or indeed all) of Grenache, Syrah and Mourvèdre in big-name regions like Bandol and Tavel (for rosé) and across southern France.

South Africa is Cinsault's home-away-from-home where as well as being widely planted for blending in Stellenbosch, it is stepping into the limelight north of Cape Town as part of the 'Swartland Revolution' (see page 114) and some single varietals are now being made.

MALBEC

Malbec stakes Argentina's claim to a place at the top table of the world's winemaking countries. It makes mighty, meaty wines that are the perfect accompaniment for the country's main activity – the consuming of beef. Seldom subtle, the best (from Luján de Cuyo, Mendoza, Salta and Tupungato) have an elemental, mineral intensity and deep damson flavours, and can be excellent value. Also known as **Côt**, it's still a big deal in parts of south-west France, especially (as **Auxerrois**) in the 'black' wines of Cahors.

MENDOZA MALBEC – STEAKING A CLAIM

Malbec has single-handedly barged Argentina's bashful winemakers onto the world's stage. It may have been dumb luck, happenstance or the work of holy fools, but somehow it found itself as the right grape in the right place at the right time. It's definitely not coincidence that the macho, meaty – even bloody – wines it makes are the perfect partner for the steaks that are the country's other pride and joy.

ONE TO DRINK

As has been the case elsewhere in the southern hemisphere and California, the youthful enthusiasm among leading producers to make exaggerated, overly intense wines with the intention of impressing wine critics and judges is on the wane. On the whole that's been a good thing, but Malbec seems well-suited to making shouty wines. Yes, they can be two-dimensional, but if those dimensions enclose a wall of flavour so intensely animal and mineral that it is experienced as something like a jolt of electric saltiness to the taste buds on the back sides of the tongue, it can be quite exhilarating. I just wouldn't want to drink it every day.

PINOTAGE

For better or worse, Pinotage is South Africa's tent-pole grape variety, being a cross between Pinot Noir and Cinsaut (which used to be called hermitage down there, hence the portmanteau name) and, until recently, you'd either love it or, more likely, leave it. It was first planted in the 1920s and spread quickly – it's a lot easier to grow than Pinot because of its thick skin.

It needs one – no other grape variety comes close to taking as much stick as Pinotage. There's a lot less talk of burnt rubber, lipstick and acetone these days and more of raspberries and spice. (That acetone thing is caused by volatile esters in case you were wondering, or are doing a pub wine quiz.). There are still some weird wines but they seem to have coalesced around 'coffee Pinotage' – a self-explanatory term once you know that heavily toasted oak staves are lobbed into the vats during maturation.

MOURVÈDRE

Known as **Mataro** in Australia and the USA and as **Monastrell** in Spain, Mourvèdre has been having a fine time of late. It has been used for ever in blends in the southern Rhône and Bandol in Provençe for adding tannic structure. But it has been in Australia – as the 'M' in fashionable, Rhône-style 'GSM' blends, along with Grenache and Shiraz – that it has finally got its name on the label, even elbowing the G off it entirely here and there.

It's similarly used in the 'Rhône Ranger' wines of California's Central Coast (see page 206), where it also makes the occasional quality single-varietal. But it's as **Monastrell** that it gets star billing in southern Spain's transformed Yecla, Jumilla and Almansa regions where plots of old vines (which nobody could afford to replace) are being gussied up by ambitious young winemakers to produce muscular, dark, tannic wines.

PETIT VERDOT

Little by name but not by nature, a splash of inky, peppery Petit Verdot goes a long way in beefing up Bordeaux blends – not just on the banks of the Gironde but wherever they are made. The grape now stands on its own two feet and makes robust single varietals in Argentina, Australia and – most promisingly – Spain's Jumilla region.

PINOT MEUNIER

Pinot Meunier is the only red grape that makes almost exclusively white wine, as the most widely planted variety in Champagne. I found a single-varietal bottling of a red in the Napa Valley once – it wasn't great wine but it was a killer in a 'name-that-grape' blind tasting.

ONE TO DRINK

AUSTRALIAN GSM BLENDS – A BEAKER FULL OF THE WARM SOUTH

Australia's recent penchant for showing its sensitive side has found its expression in wine as a turn towards subtlety and complexity from power and primary fruit.

The 'Brace yourself, Bridget!' school of winemaking is now in the hands of a serious smooth-talker. Rhône-style GSM blends (that's Grenache, Shiraz and Mourvèdre, the latter sometimes known as Mataro down-under) fit the bill to a T.

They've been spreading across the whole continent like the wildfires that have devastated large swathes of the 'traditional' Aussie plantings in recent years. Shiraz provides the throbbing black-fruit bass section, Grenache the balancing, jammy rhythm and Mourvèdre the twanging lead guitar. The inspiration for them comes from the wines of the herb-scrub slopes of the southern Rhône and such is the interconnectedness of the wine world now that some Languedoc producers now use the term GSM on their labels. You don't have to sport a beard and a beanie to drink them but it helps.

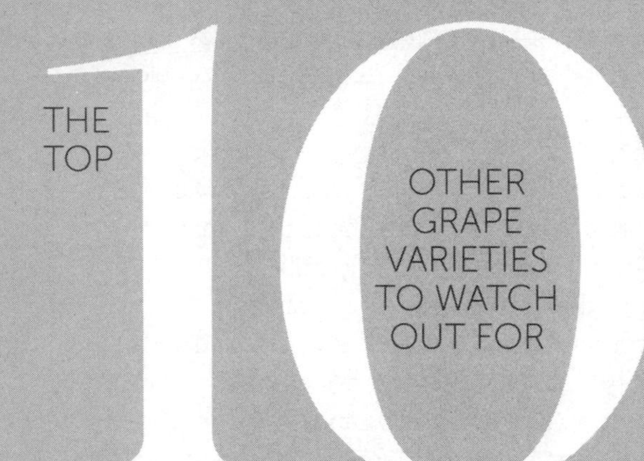

Aghiorgitiko – *Greece's silky secret weapon*

Aglianico – *grand, burly wines from southern Italy*

Baga – *big-hitter in Portugal's Bairrada*

Blaufränkisch – *savoury, spicy Austrian speciality*

Dolcetto – *light and lively north Italian*

Mencía – *succulent stuff from Spain's north-west*

Nerello Mascalese – *Sicily's answer to Beaujolais*

Nero d'Avola – *break-out volcanic reds from Sicily*

Plavac Mali – *too good for Croatia to keep it all*

Tannat – *dark and smouldering Uruguayan style*

TOURIGA NACIONAL

Touriga Nacional is the mainstay of northern Portugal's Douro region, one of the hottest, driest wine regions anywhere. Its roots can break through 15 feet of the region's slate-like schistous rocks in their search for moisture. The dark, dense, smouldering wines it makes are the mainstay in Port of all hues and qualities but – as traditional Port-drinkers are gradually sliding off their perches – some excellent winemakers are also making intense, tannic single-varietals which can be great value.

4 THE OLD AND NEW WORLDS

TEN SHORT YEARS AGO I WAS GOING TO WRITE A BOOK with a wine-columnist chum about the contrasts between 'Old World' and 'New World' wines, with one of us banging the drum for the former and the other for the latter. I'm glad it didn't happen – it would be faintly absurd now. It's all a bit more complicated than that these days and those terms seem to refer as much to ways of doing things as to where they are done.

'New World' started as a geographical term that referred to California and the southern hemisphere as far as wine – and much else – was concerned. Then it came to imply a style of very ripe, heavily extracted, upfront, fruit-forward, perhaps rather two-dimensional wines that offered power in place of complexity. It was one of those perplexing terms – like 'grammar-school boy' – that could be either pejorative or admiring depending on who uttered it.

'Old World' meant everything else and was likewise a double-edged sword. It could mean 'old-fashioned, over-regulated, out-of-touch' or 'suave, sophisticated, subtle' depending on whose lips it passed. We're a long way down the road now and there has been so much ebb and flow of influence and innovation that – blessedly – these terms are becoming obsolete and one doesn't hear them anything like as often.

Words like 'inter-connected' and 'global' have become clichés but those usually exist for a reason and, to use another, wine is very much a One World thing these days. It's as silly to dwell on anachronistic divisions within it as it would be within the world of food. Yes, we can celebrate tradition and heritage but the fact is that in my home town there's a Chilean restaurant with a Michelin star and my current favourite is run by an Aussie chef who's been fabulously fusing French and Japanese influences for 25 years, and nobody bats an eyelid.

OLD Vs NEW: A SNAPSHOT

In reality, the term 'New World' was never able to stand much analysis. Winemaking hasn't been 'new' in South Africa's Stellenbosch region for, ooh, only about 400 years (and that's 100 less than the documented history of wine in parts of South America). Australia's McLaren Vale kicked off in 1837, about the same time as California's industry got going in Sonoma.

Still, in shaping our understanding of 'New' and 'Old' World wines, the influence of the best winemakers from these 'Old New World' regions can hardly be overestimated. Courtesy of the 'flying winemaker' phenomenon of the '90s – it boomeranged back to Europe and took root. Within a decade, underperforming regions (e.g. the Languedoc, Sicily and southern and north-eastern Italy, central and north-western Spain and Greece), seldom previously responsible for anything much more than filling the EU's wine lake, were transformed into the powerhouses of the 'New Old World', producing bold, intense, fruit-driven wines to rival anything from down under. If anything, they were a little too upfront, though, and

ONE TO DRINK

THE SUPERTUSCANS – ITALY'S TRAILBLAZERS

They play a long game, the great wine families of Tuscany. Some of them have been in the business for 700 years and they know a thing or two about working the system. Starting in the late '60s some of them took against the more absurd strictures of the DOC system – which, for example, *required* a certain usage of white grapes in Chianti. They ripped up the rulebook and started growing 'international' varieties like Cabernet Sauvignon and Merlot to make fine 'Supertuscan' wines, which, as a result, they had to sell as lowly vino da tavola.

The wheel turns and those wines now sell for big money and – get this! – some of them have a DOCG of their own in Bolgheri. The 'Supertuscan' effect has been seismic and new DOCGs are springing up all along Italy's shapely thigh, between Chianti and the coast. Morellino di Scansano has been the most successful and, with the Maremma IGT, has transformed a swathe of Tuscany's lonely coastal littoral into a dynamic, some would say over-exploited, region in little more than ten years.

The original wines have attracted many wannabe, 'mini-Supertuscan', versions that go as far as (let's be charitable) riffing on the names and labelling of the top wines, but some can be excellent value. There is a common style, regardless of grape variety, which is in the 'wall of fruit' mode, a great block of it, often with coffee and chocolate notes and the trademark Italian almonds. They'd recognize the style in somewhere like the Barossa Valley, for sure, but the fruit is more stewed than primary. I dare say it all seemed very New World in the '80s and '90s but I'm not quite sure what it is now – the 'Old New Old World', maybe?

all those super-ripe blackcurrant fruit gums started to seem a little clumsy – 'alcoholic fruit juice' was the complaint on everybody's lips.

WINEMAKING IN THE 21ST CENTURY: A BRAVE NEW WORLD

What went around came around and then it went round again such that now – in the 'New New World' – there are far fewer blockbusting, over-powered single varietals and the whole world is moving towards a lighter, subtler approach. What a relief. Much of this has been achieved by focusing on the extreme latitudes at which grapes will ripen but you can get the same effect from going up as well as away. There's been a huge uplift in making wines at higher altitude. This '3D-winemaking' is delivering bright, balanced wines from vines grown on slopes everywhere from the South American Andes to Sicily's Mount Etna, and from the American Pacific North-West via South Africa and New Zealand to sites all over Australia.

There's also much more blending going on these days and, guess what? Much of it picks up on what they've been doing back in the Old Old World for centuries. How about adding a little (white) Viognier to soften out your booming Aussie Syrah? That's the trick in Côte-Rôtie in the northern Rhône. Looking to add some more complexity to your red by splashing in some

THE REAL WINE REVOLUTION

Rather than getting bogged down with the terms 'Old' and 'New' world, the best way to get your head around the most exciting things that are happening in today's edgy world of winemaking is to look right there – at the edges. There's always been something special about wine from the cool-climate zones at the limits of where grapes will fully ripen – think of Champagne, Burgundy, Piedmont and the Rhine for starters – and the magic is that the grapes retain the thrill of acidity that gives them freshness and vibrancy. In a word, edge.

If you want to know about climate change, by the way, ask a cool-climate winemaker. Those edges are shifting around all over the place and sites that would have been beyond the pale even five or ten years ago are now very much in play. They know, for example, that the extraordinary rise of English sparkling wine – which can now rival Champagne for quality – is no fluke.

Grenache and Mourvèdre? That's always been the way in the southern Rhône. And as for toning down overly fruity Cabernet Sauvignon with Merlot or Cabernet Franc, well, there's not much you can teach the Bordelais about that. But people are riffing too – how about trying that Côte-Rôtie trick by adding some spicy white Torrontés to a beefy Malbec? They're doing that in Argentina and calling it 'Malbrontés'. It's a full-time job just keeping up.

With the exception of the most traditional of European enclaves, the old certainties about which grape varieties are grown where no longer apply. Those certainties were all too often accompanied by an equal amount of provincialism and prejudicial lumber, so it's no bad thing. The changes have been wholesale, to the extent that it has seemed at times in the last 20 years that everybody wanted to grow everything, everywhere. That runaway proliferation is now slowing as it becomes clearer which bets have paid off.

Only a brave or demented punter would have laid a three-way accumulator that fussy, finicky Pinot Noir – once, to all intents and purposes, only to be found in France's Burgundy region – would thrive as well in parts of Romania as it also now does in Tasmania and in New Zealand's Central Otago region. And in Germany, for that matter, where some regions now make more red wine than white – and yes, I did say Germany. It's a funny old (new) world.

REVOLUTIONARY WINE REGIONS

Mount Etna, Sicily

For making mysterious wines with acidity and brimstone minerality. . . on a rumbling volcano!

Swartland, South Africa

For smart, experienced winemakers tearing up the rule book with their red blends (see page 114).

Yarra Valley, Australia

A while back people thought Pinot Noir could only thrive in Burgundy but here demonstrates otherwise.

Pic St-Loup, Languedoc, France

For making (alongside its' neighbours in La Clape and Pézenas) wild and wonderful wines in wild and wonderful places.

Central Coast Region, California

For throwing off the Napa yoke and making fresh, bright wines from everything you can think of (see page 106).

ONE TO DRINK

PINOT NOIR FROM . . . ALL POINTS SOUTH

Many of the world's great wines are blends – after all, it's about balance and harmony so it makes sense. But there's another aspect to balance that can involve one grape just as much as a bunch of different ones. It can be about getting the right result from how and where the grapes are grown just as much as it can be about what they're made into.

Pinot used to be considered as one of the most difficult grapes to grow successfully. It turns out it wasn't difficult; it just has very high standards. As such, it's the mark of talented winemakers – and, increasingly, a talented winemaking country – to demonstrate they can meet its demands. Little Red Riding-Hood likes it not too hot and not too cold, but just right.

There are many such winemakers now, and, whether they're in California's Sonoma or Chile's Leyda Valley, New Zealand's Central Otago region, the wilds of Tasmania or South Africa's Western Cape, they know how to make fresh-faced, scented, strawberryish wines. Warmer climates make for bigger wines and these may have broader shoulders than their privileged cousins in Burgundy, but they have poise and polish and just enough of everything, and never too much of anything. They're just right. Well done, everybody.

5 FRANCE

FRANCE MAY BE AN ECONOMIC BASKET-CASE-IN-WAITING where over 50% of GDP is spent – to all intents and purposes – on subsidising the ruminations of 66 million *soi-disant* philosophers, but the French still have their own unique and irreplaceable national genius and in nothing does it better express itself than their wine. It's the mission control, the Pantheon, the Xanadu of wine but, as with their food, it's changing as fast as you can say 'McDonald's' and – whisper it – your typical Brit now knows more about wine than the average Frenchman does.

BORDEAUX

No ifs, no buts – Bordeaux is the world's greatest red wine region. Cabernet Sauvignon and Merlot are the kingpins, supported mainly by Cabernet Franc and Petit Verdot, making complex, age-worthy wines for grown-ups. The cost of a single bottle of the very best stuff would put an average-priced bottle of wine on the table every day for a year.

The pecking order in Bordeaux is a strict one – there has always been a lot of money at stake. On the left bank (of the river Gironde, which divides the region) the five 'first growths' are at the very top of the tree of 61 classed-growth (*cru classé*) producers. The classification was made in 1855 and only one very prestigious château has muscled its way into the club since, in 1973. Properties are ranked from first to fifth growths and – to

THE TOP 10 BORDEAUX VILLAGES

Fronsac
Listrac
Margaux
Moulis
Pauillac
Pessac-Léognan
Pomerol
St-Émilion
St-Estèphe
St-Julien

be fair – it remains a surprisingly accurate guide to quality and price. Next come the 250 or so *crus bourgeois* (yes, really – soooo French!) and then the 8,000-odd unpredictable *petits châteaux*.

There are more rules, of course – we're in France – so the vast majority of the billion or so bottles made in the region can only be labelled 'AOP Bordeaux'. (That's *Appellation d'Origine Protégée*, which has replaced the old *Appellation d'Origine Contrôlée* classification.). Labels saying *Bordeaux Supérieur*, the next rank up, may well be worth a try (while those declaring themselves as *Grand Vin de Bordeaux* are usually fibbing). Thankfully, the focus narrows when the place names get more specific. Bottles showing the district, e.g. **Médoc** (and more especially **Haut-Médoc**), **Graves** and **Premières Côtes de Bordeaux** have potential and there is not much wine that is either bad or cheap that has the precise village cited on the label (see previous page).

On the right bank, Merlot is the star in **St-Émilion**, which has a somewhat less complicated and much less reliable ranking system. There are a baker's dozen of fabulous *premiers grands crus classés*, 55 variable *grands crus classés* and finally hundreds of *grand crus*, many of which are not that *grand* at all. Democratic **Pomerol** has no pecking order and makes bold, fruity, modern wines, some of which are among the most expensive of all (and outlying **Lalande de Pomerol** is worth trying for mini-me versions). More good value is to be had from the **Côte de Castillon** and **Côte de Bourg**, **Blaye-Côtes-de Bordeaux** and, further afield, **Bergerac**.

BURGUNDY

At least the grapes (or, rather, grape) is simple in Burgundy, because nothing else is – Pinot Noir is basically it for reds. Unthinkable 20 years ago, Pinot now makes gluggable – and sometimes glorious – wine the world over, but the Côte d'Or isn't called 'Golden' for nothing. (It's not a name you'll ever see on a label, though; it just refers jointly to the two best, most central areas, the **Côte de Nuits** and the **Côte de Beaune.**)

Even the names of Burgundy's great wine villages (see page 82) have a rich and silky mouth-feel to them, and bottles with labels that proudly show the name of any of these places are always expensive... although not in comparison to those that show the names of the tiny, hallowed individual vineyards of the *premiers* and *grands crus* within them such as **Le Musigny**, **Chambertin**, **Corton** and **La Romanée-Conti**, which are among the most expensive in the world.

The second-tier villages of the Côte d'Or have upped their game greatly in recent years and names like **Savigny-lès-Beaune**, **St-Aubin**, **Pernand-Vergelesses**, **Santenay**, **Fixin**, **Monthélie**, **Marsannay**, **Auxey-Duresses** and **Saint-Romain** give a glimpse of the glory – and they don't sound too shabby either, do they?

Indeed, standards throughout the region have improved so much that a peek through the window can sometimes be had from the wines labelled Côte or Hautes-Côtes de Nuits or Beaune and especially Côte de Nuits-Villages, which can be made from a blend of wines from strictly defined areas. Plain *Bourgogne Rouge* is more of a gamble, but some of the top producers and blenders (*negoçiants*) make good things from carefully selected wines.

ONE TO DRINK

CLARET – WHAT MOST WINE WANTS TO BE WHEN IT GROWS UP

Let's get one thing straight: 'claret' means any red wine from Bordeaux, nothing more and nothing less. But (and I'm really sorry about this) it's a word you'll only usually find on a supermarket own-brand label and is, as such, completely useless.

It's not surprising the British have always had a fondness for claret – the whole region was under English rule for the best part of three centuries in the middle ages – and there are still masses of Brits involved in all aspects of the wine trade in Bordeaux. We pinched the word 'claret' from the Spanish. Their own red wines (called *tinto* – which also means ink) were so inky-dark that they used their name for rosé – *clarete* – to describe their French neighbours' lighter style of reds.

Much claret is bog-standard, but you get what you pay for and the good stuff is the gold standard, the *ne plus ultra* of red wine. Happily, a glimpse round the door can be had for as little as three times the average cost of a bottle of wine. And what can you hope to get for your money? Well, the typical blackcurrant Cabernet Sauvignon fruit is now stewed with roasted spices, and the effect is something like a rich and mature fruit cake. If your luck's in or, more likely, somebody has stumped up double that money, you should get some of that cedar cigar box aroma that I was talking about and an intensity of flavour that lingers on your taste buds for a minute or so. Double up again, and maybe there'll be something even lovelier and more ethereal and inimitable floating above everything else... like violets.

THE TOP 10 BURGUNDY VILLAGES

Aloxe-Corton
Beaune
Chambolle-Musigny
Gevrey-Chambertin
Morey-St-Denis
Nuits-St-Georges
Pommard
Volnay
Vosne-Romanée
Vougeot

RHÔNE

The folk of the Rhône Valley have no truck with elitist *cru* systems and the like. Their pecking order is more deeply ingrained. There is no cheap and little bad wine from the northern villages of **Crozes-Hermitage**, **Cornas**, **St-Joseph** and – grandest of all – **Côte-Rôtie** and **Hermitage** (see page 44), which all devote themselves exclusively to the Syrah grape. Crozes is the entry point price-wise and its peppery, spicy, meaty wines might give you a taste for the big stuff but be warned: these wines demand as much from your patience as they do from your purse – some can be barely drinkable under ten years of age.

The south, where they make ten times as much wine from a plethora of grape varieties, could not be more different. Fruity, jammy Grenache is the mainstay in blends where Syrah and Mourvèdre are important in stiffening and spicing it up and Cinsaut and Counoise also play useful roles. Of the vast output of Côtes du Rhône, careful digging can unearth some great-value wines – often designated Côtes du Rhône-Villages and preferably with the mention of a specific village, e.g. **Cairanne**, **Rasteau**, **Sablet** and **Plan de Dieu** – evocative of stewed fruits and the crackle of herb-scrub *garrigue* underfoot.

More good, sun-baked value is to be had in southern Rhône appellations like **Coteaux du Tricastin**, **Costières de Nîmes** and **Ventoux**. Moving upscale, as prices have been lately, **Vacqueyras** and **Gigondas** are the places to get a sense of the rambunctious, thigh-slapping, age-worthy, food-friendly reds of Châteauneuf-du-Pape – the undisputed pontiff of the southern Rhône and one of the world's great red wines (see page 22).

REST OF FRANCE

Gamay – the poor man's Pinot Noir – rules the roost in **Beaujolais**. The names of the villages – Brouilly, Côte-de-Brouilly, Chénas, Chiroubles, Fleurie, Juliénas, Morgon, Moulin-à-Vent, Régnié, St-Amour – are almost as seductive as those of its northern cousins in Burgundy, and labels showing the name of any one of them are what to look for. Standards have risen so far and so fast that even generic *Beaujolais-Villages*, blended wines sourced from a number of them may safely be approached, but anything lower, i.e. straight *Beaujolais*, risks a reminder of the bad old days.

All along the **Loire**, in places with lovely names like Chinon, Saumur-Champigny and St-Nicolas-de-Bourgeuil, fruity reds that have always been especially popular in Paris as the local wines are made from Cabernet Franc, Gamay and Pinot Noir. They can be pinky pale or inky dark but they all share the freshness and minerality you'd expect this far north (only ghostly pale Alsace Pinot Noir is further up the map.)

It's a fair generalization to say that the further south you go the bigger the wines you find. In the far South-West, a taste of the 'black' wines of **Cahors** (made from Côt, i.e. Malbec), the **Pays Basque**, **Collioure** and **Madiran** (made from Tannat) prove the point better than any description can. Much good wine that used to be labelled Vin de Pays is to be had from the south, only it's now clunkily called Indication Géographique Protégée (IGP).

Further east, into **Roussillon** and the **Languedoc** is France's own new world. Some of the old names – Fitou, Faugères,

Corbières and Minervois – have transformed themselves in order to compete with the new ones, like Côtes Catalanes, Pic St-Loup, St-Chinian and La Clape. There are world class winemakers in these places now, revelling in the freedom from over-regulation and making wines from all sorts of grapes, but all with a streak of mountain wildness to them.

The Côtes de Provence stretches up to 100 miles east of the Rhône and it's best to look for one of the smaller AOP regions like Les Baux-en-Provence, Lubéron, or Coteaux Varois, where cooler temperatures make for fresher wines. Best of all, Bandol is Provence's flag-carrier for long-lived, meaty, mineral, herb-edged reds made mainly from Mourvèdre. **Corsica** is for rugged, rustic reds that round the castle run.

FLEURIE – BY NAME AND BY NATURE

ONE TO DRINK

Fleurie is one of the ten village crus of Beaujolais and not a million miles away from Burgundy in style (or, for that matter, by road – it's next door, to the south). Beaujolais has transformed itself in the last ten years and although the Gamay grape doesn't lay claim to any great complexity (at least not when young), what it does well, it does very well. It makes quintessentially summery wines brimming with youthful vigour and flirtatiousness. The flavours are of cherry-ripeness and a glass of bright, tight Fleurie should make one want to frolic around a maypole in a gingham frock.

Beaujolais has a lot of previous to atone for. The annual fiasco of Beaujolais Nouveau Day every November in the '80s and '90s, in which people raced from the region at midnight on the third Wednesday to see who could be first to serve the frequently foul, just-fermented, lip-staining new vintage, has taken a generation to live down. But that's all in the past, so pop the flowery one in the fridge for half-an-hour (a little kiss of coldness gives it a crisp, even somehow crunchy edge) and take it on a picnic with somebody *ravissant*.

6 THE REST OF EUROPE

THERE IS NOTHING THAT CAN BE DONE WITH THE fermented juice of black grapes that isn't done with it somewhere in Europe. There is everything from sparkling, pinky-pale flibbertigibbets to table-thumping, black wines you can't see a light bulb through – and everything imaginable in between. It would be a crime not to take more than the occasional dip into some of the less familiar waters of this great ocean of diversity. From the Douro to the Danube, the imagination, expense and effort that go into putting some of even the lowliest-priced bottles on our tables are at a level never known before. Explore! Enjoy!! Hallelujah Europa!!!

ITALY

Only Italy comes close to France in terms of diversity. They grow nearly 1,000 different grape varieties in 500 different *denominazioni* and every now and again a wine shows up that hasn't been seen for years. It's best to carve the boot up into four – the cuffs of the north-west and north-east, the central shin and calf and the southerly foot.

The key to the north-west – **Piedmont** and **Lombardy** – is the three Bs: Barolo and Barbaresco; which make beautiful reds from the Nebbiolo grape in a myriad of microscopic vineyards the names of which I can never remember, and the Barbera grape which makes lighter, easier-drinking reds. The finest, fabulously expensive *riserva* wines require five years of ageing in Barolo and four in Barabaresco but a sniff of the glory can be had from the relatively lowly Langhe Nebbiolo, Valtellina, Gattinara and Carema demarcations. Dolcetto, Brachetto, Grignolino and Freisa provide other lighter wines (and I like saying the names).

Over to the north-east, in the **Veneto, Friuli-Venezia Giulia** and way up north in the mountainous **Trentino-Alto Adige**, which borders Austria, the reds are generally fresh and light – Valpolicella and Bardolino are the two biggest names. Amarone, made from semi-dried grapes, is the honourable exception – it's one of the biggest wines made anywhere (see overleaf). There are lots of 'international' grapes grown but lots of indigenous ones – and more marvellous names – too: Marzemino, Refosco, Teroldego Rotaliano.

Sangiovese is king in the central part of the country, in **Tuscany** and **Umbria** – it's the grape that makes, for better or worse, Italy's most famous wine, Chianti. Chianti Classico is a step up in quality and if the label says *riserva* it means the wine has been aged for up to three years before release. Others of Italy's grandest Sangiovese reds are from these parts as well, Brunello di Montalcino and Vino Nobile di Montepulciano among them and Carmignano provides a low-cost introduction to the style.

International varieties are used for the 'Supertuscans' that threw away the rule book and had to be labelled *vino da tavola*, and some of them now even have their own DOCGs. At the other end of the scale, there are often excellent-value wines classified

ONE TO DRINK

AMARONE DELLA VALPOLICELLA – ALL ABOUT THAT BASS

People who associate the name Valpolicella with the tart, thin wines that characterized much of the area's output until very recently might be surprised to know that the pride and joy of the region, burly Amarone, is unquestionably one of the greatest and costliest red wines of Italy. The first one I tried came as a shock, not least because of the alcohol content (which – at 15% – was off the clock). The wines are made from super-ripe grapes (mainly Corvina) which are semi-dried, a process that concentrates the flavours into an essence of bitter cherry and dark-chocolate loveliness.

These are wines for partnering the biggest, richest food – the name itself means 'big bitter one' but the sweetness of the fruit, intensified by dehydration, keeps everything in balance, except the price. As such, it's worth looking out for wines labelled Ripasso di Valpolicella Classico (or, better yet, Superiore) – the leftover skins from the making of sweet Recioto wines are resourcefully added to regular Valpolicella during fermentation to give extra body resulting, with luck, in good-value, mini-Amarones.

as IGT (Indicazione Geografica Protteta) – Italy's equivalent of what used to be called Vin de Pays in France.

The south is the place for easy-going, rustic wines and quality is improving rapidly. The **Abruzze** has sometimes elegant Montepulciano (as in the grape, not the place – sorry, but we're in Italy) while **Puglia**, the ankle and heel, is catching up fast with powerful Primitivo and Negroamaro blends.

There are lovely, complex reds made from Aglianico in Taurasi in the **Campania** region, north of la bella Napoli and in **Basilicata** along the instep. **Sicily** is Italy's new world, making some exciting stuff, especially from volcanic Nero d'Avola and Nerello Mascalese on the super-duper trendy slopes of Etna and lighter, Beaujolais-like Frapatto.

SPAIN

There are many contenders, but Spain shades it as the most-improved wine country in the last few years and it is ticking all the boxes. Because nobody could afford to replace them, they already had lots of old vines, many of them of 'rediscovered' grape varieties like Mencía, Graciano, Bobal, Juan García and loads more very few people have ever heard of – there are now more than 100 being grown commercially in total.

Spain has its own new world, both in rejuvenated, traditional red regions like **Bierzo**, **Jumilla**, **Yecla**, and **Toro** (and the list doesn't stop there, by a long chalk) and in new, large, loosely-regulated central areas like **Castilla y León** where sparky winemakers are able to do more or less what they like. Having already clicked with the idea that lower yields make better wine, they coupled that with improved practice in the winery, and – given that many of these wines are exceedingly good value – the place has taken off like a rocket.

The hot centre is home to both grand, bold reds from **Ribera del Duero** and high-quality everyday drinkers from **Valdepeñas** while fascinating things are happening around the coastal edges with Monastrell (Mourvèdre) in **Alicante**, with Garnacha (Grenache) in **Priorat** and inland with Carignan in **Cariñena** and Tempranillo in **Campo de Borja** and more Garnacha in **Calatayud**.

There's just one worrying thing and that is that in **Rioja** (see overleaf) – still Spain's premier wine region and home to one of the greatest and most distinctive wine styles anywhere – the traditional, elegant, silky, vanilla-scented, American-oak-aged wines are rapidly disappearing in favour of intense, fruit-forward, young styles to the extent that only a handful of producers are still making them.

RIOJA GRAN RESERVA – AGE AND BEAUTY

ONE TO DRINK

A bit like Chianti, Rioja is such a large and diverse region that, apart from the main permitted grape varieties themselves – chiefly Tempranillo, supported by Grenache (called Mazuelo here) and sometimes a bit of Graciano – there is no single aspect in common for all the red wines that have the word Rioja on the label. Odd, then, that the *reserva* (one year's ageing in cask and two years in bottle) and *gran reserva* wines (two and three years respectively) from the traditional producers are about the closest that wine ever gets to coming with a guarantee of quality.

What is guaranteed – especially with the *gran reservas* - is an object lesson in the beneficial effects of age on fermented grape juice. The casks are American oak and deliver the distinctive sweet vanilla notes that are the perfect counterpoint to the spice-drawer, cherry-compôte flavours, and the overall effect is of elegant, decadent ripeness in decay.

PORTUGAL

Portugal appears to have kept a close eye on what is happening to the east and north and improvements here are of a comparable order of magnitude. Portuguese reds, like so many Italian ones, seem to have a common thread, something like an accent, and here it's about a brambly intensity and minerality that are major assets.

The famous **Dão** region – Portugal's Rioja, or maybe Barolo – is gradually rehabilitating itself after decades in the doldrums and is making ethereal, perfumed wines from Alfrocheiro, Touriga Nacional, Tinta Roriz and Jaen (aka Mencía in Spain). Neighbouring **Bairrada** is now making wines of equal quality from the promising Baga variety and the **Douro** is already well-established for strapping, dinner-party reds (see overleaf). Portugal's new world is dotted about in its newer Vino Regional appellations like the **Alantejo** and **Lisboa**, and, within them, small high-quality DOCs **Beira Interior**, **Alenquer**, **Palmela** and **Portalegre** where quality-focused producers are waiting in the wings.

GERMANY, AUSTRIA, GREECE AND EASTERN EUROPE

It might take a while but the red wines of **Germany** will grow on you. The best are from Spätburgunder (Pinot Noir) mainly from the Ahr and Baden Württemberg regions, with good ones also popping up around the Pfalz and Rheingau. They're pinky pale but there's plenty of depth and sinewy complexity in the best of them, helped along with some judicious oak. Fuller-bodied wines are made from Dornfelder and Lemberger (Austria's Blaufränkisch).

Austria has its own style – bold, bright and brash. Primary, purple damson fruit with serious minerality and acidity abounds – they're seldom cheap but they're often good value. Blaufränkisch, Zweigelt and St-Laurent are the grapes to look for and Burgenland is where they thrive.

Greece has found a way to keep the natural tendency towards over-ripeness – that baked, or, worse yet, burnt-rubber thing – in check most of the time. At their best from Nemea in the Naoussa region, perfumed wines from Xinomavro and powerful, oak-aged ones from Aghiorgitiko can be world-class.

The winemaking countries of south-eastern Europe – notably **Hungary**, **Romania**, **Slovenia**, **Croatia** and **Macedonia** – are sleeping giants. They are, however, slowly waking up to the fact that world wants less, but better, wine. They can all make excellent stuff from fascinating indigenous grapes when they want to, but can they do it at a price the rest of the world wants to pay?

DOURO – HIGH AND MIGHTY

ONE TO DRINK

The concept of a 'field blend' is enough to give a techie, tyro winemaker the heebie-jeebies. Basically, it means that the growers don't know exactly what grapevines they have. More euphemistically referred to as 'mixed plantings', they are surprisingly common in the high, hot fastnesses of the dry Douro Valley where – to be blunt – nobody had the money to rip out the indigenous varieties during the Cabernet Sauvignonization of the '80s and '90s.

It's an ill wind, as they say, and this being Port country, there'll be lots of Touriga Nacional, Tinta Roriz (Spain's Tempranillo) and Touriga Francesa and plenty more besides to the extent that every now again the boffins turn up a previously unknown variety. In an age in which Port's rambunctious style is a little at odds with the zeitgeist, the top producers (the 'Douro Boys') are turning a lot of their production into table – rather than fortified – wines.

You'd expect a wine that is basically unfortified Port to be rich, robust and complex and you wouldn't be disappointed. There's something else as well – a seam of deep minerality and a streak of wildness worthy only of grapes that know they can survive in what is possibly the most hostile of all the environments in which they are grown.

7 USA AND THE SOUTHERN HEMISPHERE

THERE'S NOTHING THAT EUROPEAN WINEMAKERS haven't done with the fermented juice of black grapes and there's nothing that they do with it to which the rest of the world doesn't say: 'Nice. But how about if we just tried . . .' This two-way traffic seems, right now, like a virtuous circle running in both directions. I don't want to sound like a recent recruit to some wide-eyed, wallet-wasting cult but – whatever the mass media is telling you – we twenty-first centurians are fortunate to live in an unprecedented, golden age of peace, prosperity and progress and what is happening with wine is just one little bit of it. But it's one that – for anybody prepared to expend the small efforts necessary to take advantage of it – makes every day (except Mondays) that little bit better.

USA & MEXICO

There are wineries in all 50 states of the Union but it's almost impossible to avoid using the terms 'Californian' and 'American' interchangeably where wine is concerned. So here's to the Pacific North-west – **Oregon** and **Washington** – where they only make good wine (apart from great wine) as far as I can tell, and from just about every major variety you could shake a stick at.

'**California**' doesn't mean '**Napa Valley**' either, but the gravitational pull is irresistibly strong. It's a different world, a pampered agricultural theme park where I have totted up that the average (yes, average) bottle of Cabernet Sauvignon in a leading wine merchant in Yountville is ten times the price of our average bottle of wine.

A lot of these small-production, so-called 'garage' wines, often seem over-extracted as well as overpriced to most European tastes, but the main market for them is within California itself and they seldom escape that gravity. The best of the bigger names are often made in the image of modern claret but there's usually better value to be had from Bordeaux.

Those wines get the headlines, but California – and Napa – is diverse. There are good value 'CalItalian' wines, made from Sangiovese, Barbera and Nebbiolo in **Sonoma** and characterful wines made by the dedicated group of 'Rhône Rangers'. Serious quality is also to be had from **Carneros** (especially Pinot Noir) and serious value from the **Central Coast** region, not to be confused with the **Central Valley**, where the bulk agribusiness stuff comes from (although there are better subregions like **Lodi** within it).

The fact that there is fine wine to be had from **Texas**, **Virginia** and **New York State** is one to tuck away until you're in the land of the free as the little that is exported is necessarily expensive. Further south, winemakers in **Mexico** turn out some good, bold reds from Zinfandel and Petite Syrah (no relation) especially in the long finger of land called the Baja California peninsula.

ONE TO DRINK

CENTRAL COAST, CALIFORNIA – THE SANTA CLAUSE

California, for most wine drinkers, is the most polarized wine region in the world. At one extreme there are the expensive – and often fabulous – wines of the Northern Coast (centred around the Napa Valley and Sonoma) and, at the other, the lumpen, lowest-common-denominator stuff from the irrigated desert that is the Central Valley.

They drink a lot of wine in California and the fact that more people don't know about the Central Coast is that they keep the vast bulk of it for themselves. It's a vast region, stretching from the Santa Cruz Mountains area just south of San Francisco for 250 miles down to Santa Barbara. Within it there are a tangled muliplicity of subregions and climates in which they grow a huge variety of grapes.

In short, it's a mini-Europe. The unifying aspect amid all the diversity is the Pacific Ocean. Cool is a relative term when applied to weather but it's an absolute when applied to a winemaker. The Pacific breezes (and fog in the north) is what keeps everything fresh and bright, with clarity of flavour, poise and good acidity. The wine-speak term is 'lifted'.

Cabernet Sauvignon from the Santa Rita Valley and Zin from Paso Robles don't sound too ground-breaking, I know, so try some Sangiovese from the Santa Ynez Valley, some Barbera, Pinot Noir or pretty much anything from the Santa Maria Valley (where they grow pretty much everything) and, indeed, from any of the other Sans and Santas. The only problem is getting your hands on some.

AUSTRALIA

Australian winemakers did more to change the landscape of wine in the last two decades of the twentieth century than those of all of the rest of the world combined. They made wine democratic and made it OK for geezers and blokes to drink it, not just chaps. Then the wheels fell off. The wines started to look like overblown caricatures and they made too much of them.

It all got a bit biblical after that with droughts, bush fires and bankruptcies, but Aussies are as tough as old secateurs – turning all that experience towards an understated, balanced and, yes, I'll say it, elegant product, delivered with a knowing wink. If you think you know Australian wine and don't like it, think again.

Yes, the classic regions that made Australia's name – the **Barossa Valley**, **Coonawarra** and **McLaren Vale** chief among them – are still going great guns but even they have turned the volume down somewhat in terms of style. Yes, there's still plenty of dull beverage wine (just called 'juice' in Aussie winemaker parlance) from the vast, irrigated desert of the Murray-Darling basin but almost everywhere else the 'new new world' is at hand.

Adelaide Hills, **Langhorne Creek**, **Mornington Peninsula**, **Wrattonbully**, **Heathcote** and the whole of **Tasmania** are some of the places where the cool kids congregate. That's cool as in climate – either coastal or in climbing to altitudes where ripeness comes with a jolt of acidity guaranteed to balance things and keep everything fresh.

The **Yarra Valley** is where the old and the new cross-pollinate, and in truth they've been quietly doing a lot of this stuff out in

Western Australia for ages, but the cool kids know everything and grow everything and they can do it on the cheap – and if it isn't fabulous they rip it up and start again. Pinot Noir is the *grape du jour*, with GSM blends for warmer spots, but they're working with every grape variety you've ever heard of and when they really crack Nebbiolo and Tempranillo there will be some very worried winemakers back in the old countries.

NEW ZEALAND

Kiwis could even teach their Aussie neighbours a thing or two about resourcefulness and a general can-do attitude, but everybody makes mistakes. Kiwis took ages and a few false starts to work out that Pinot Noir would be their red counterpart to Sauvignon Blanc. There are pockets of good Syrah, Cab Sauv, Merlot and much else besides here and there in the hands of quality producers, but Pinot is the grape with the kerr-ching factor.

Chilly **Central Otago** – the most southerly wine region anywhere – on the South Island is the crucible but Pinot has made inroads everywhere, even into the Sauvignon-Central region of **Marlborough.** Other good places are **Martinborough**, **Waipara**, **Wairarapa** and the **Waitaki and Wairau Valleys.** Lots of people are starting to make Champagne-style sparkling wines – handy in the unlikely event that Pinot-fatigue should eventually set in.

ONE TO DRINK

BAROSSA SHIRAZ – DARK AND STORMY

There's one little patch of Shiraz vines in the Barossa Valley – Australia's Napa – that dates back to 1843 and is among the oldest plantings of any grape variety anywhere. So how much sense it makes to refer in this case to a 'new world' style I'm not quite sure, but the Barossa certainly makes distinctive wines. The ancient root systems burrow deep enough not to require irrigation during the long, hot summers (they're 'dry-farmed' in the buzz-phrase).

These old vines make the deeply concentrated, chocolatey, brooding style that is the Barossa's unique selling point. Thankfully, the happy Aussie knack of mingling tradition and modernity is never far away, though, and there's another buzz around the area's Côte-Rôtie-style blends – traditional in the northern Rhône – which add a splash of fragrant, white Viognier to lift the spirits of the sometimes overwrought, even medicinal, Shiraz.

We know that Shiraz is Syrah and vice-versa, and it just depends on whether you're in France or not, don't we? Yes, but in a mildly mind-bending development of nominative determinism, southern hemisphere makers of lighter, more balanced styles of Shiraz, often with the freshness and acidity that comes from growing at greater altitude (or latitude), are now calling it Syrah. So what, really, is in a name?

SOUTH AMERICA

Chile's wine has grown up in the last few years and much can be said in favour of its increasingly poised and polished early adulthood. There is a history of vines that goes back to the conquistadores but it's only 20 years since it walked out onto the world's stage.

Cabernet Sauvignon, Merlot and latterly Carmenère have been top of the class for reds for ages but things are changing fast. Syrah with a light touch in cooler regions and Pinot Noir grown at altitude are the future. In buzzy regions like **Aconcagua Costa**, **Bío-Bío**, **Elqui**, **Limarí** and **Tabalí** other Southern French grapes – Cab Franc, Grenache, Mourvèdre and Carignan – and Italian varieties are also making headway as winemakers the world over realize they have to pay as much attention to finding the next big thing as they do to financing the current one.

Argentina has sensibly been looking ahead to the day when people might tire of Malbec and mostly they've been looking upwards. They have some of the highest vineyards in the world in the **Uco Valley** and in **Salta** (especially the **Calchaquí Valley** at over 2,500m) – as well as some of the most southerly in **Rio Negro** – which makes for crisper, cleaner styles of Syrah, Cab Sauv and now Petit Verdot than the sweltering lowlands.

The main region of **Mendoza** is becoming less of a Malbec monoculture with Pinot Noir and northern Italian varieties (Bonarda and Corvina among them) showing clean-cut promise. All of which is not to say that a mighty Malbec doesn't have its place. It does and it's usually a few inches away from a piece of rare red meat (with which few wines work a more sinuous tango).

SOUTH AFRICA

Probably more of the wines that have demonstrated the seismic nature of the changes in the world's wine landscape have come from South Africa than anywhere else. OK, so a lot of them have been white but the reds also show that the right grapevine planted in the right place – especially if it has been in the ground a long time – is far more likely to produce exciting wine than the most fashionable grape planted a few years ago just any-old-where.

The stuff from ancient, straggly, low-yielding bush vines of something un-starry like Cinsault, Grenache, even Pinotage, has the complexity and breadth and minerality that only deep roots can winkle out from the good earth. Of course most production of the Springboks' booming industry isn't like this, but this book is about the interesting stuff that's worth the effort of finding (and, if needs be, paying for).

Some of the wines from those gnarly old vines are made in the big-ticket, traditional areas like **Stellenbosch**, **Paarl** and **Franschhoek.** Some are made in South's own 'new new world', in sea-breezy **Elgin**, **Elim** and **Hemel-en-Aarde** and in sun-bleached **Swartland** (see overleaf). Some of these game-changing wines are expensive but some are less than twice the cost of our average bottle... and if that's not seismic, then what on earth is?

ONE TO DRINK

SWARTLAND – THE REVOLUTION IS AT HAND

I bang on a lot about the ebb and flow of influences and ideas back and forth (and back again) between the old world and the new world (and not a little about how brittle those terms have in themselves become). A lot of this flighty stuff comes firmly in to land in the once-obscure area of hot (but ocean-breezy) Swartland, inland from South Africa's western coast.

The climate is Mediterranean and so are the grapes. The land is – or was – cheap. Lots of old, low-yielding, unirrigated bush-vines have been lovingly rehabilitated to bring forth small quantities of intense juice that has plenty of acidity to keep everything fresh. There's some Cinsault and Syrah, probably some Grenache and Mourvèdre, maybe even some Cabernet Sauvignon and other bits and bobs.

The wine is complex, ripe (but not over-ripe) with plenty of minerality and the whole harmonious effect is not dissimilar to the best wines of the southern Rhône. Funny that. What goes around comes around, then goes around again. Fabulous wine doesn't necessarily need a fancy name (or a fancy price) any more.

8 BUYING RED WINE

CONSIDER THE 'AVERAGE' BOTTLE OF WINE. IT COSTS very little – about the same as a large glass of wine or a pint of beer in a city centre pub. It might be from somewhere like 'South Eastern Australia' – a term so vague that it could be from anywhere (and everywhere) down under except the far, far west. If so, the vines may have been grown hydroponically (or as near as makes no difference) in a desert. It might have had toasted oak chips floating about in it at some point to give it a veneer of barrel ageing. It may also have had some tweaking with added sugar to plump it up or with acidity to slim it down... or maybe a bit of both, just to be on the safe side. It may well have been imported in a tanker and bottled on an industrial estate. And you know what? It will probably taste... perfectly pleasant.

Buying wine has never been this painless; it's hard to buy a bad bottle these days – by which I mean the sort of stuff we drank in the '70s and '80s and that only an unshakeable intent upon inebriation could mitigate. Back then, if you wanted anything better, even splashing out was no guarantee of anything other than more plonk but with a fancier name. Many of that generation, egged-on by the 'why pay more – it all tastes the same?' mentality of wine guides like *Superplonk* are still licking the wounds of all those disappointments. Low expectation gets what it deserves.

WHERE TO BUY

The problem is that the vast bulk of wine sold by the supermarkets for consumption the same day is simply *too cheap*. Things are not so bad in the big wine-producing countries, but in Northern Europe the very high rates of government duty and sales tax mean that the actual contents of an average-priced bottle of wine typically account for less than 10% of the cost. Aside from the tax, the rest goes on bottling, labelling, packing, shipping and marketing.

Worse yet, it's such a ferociously competitive sector that profit margins are way too tight for any hopeful drinker to realistically expect much more than the lowest common denominator from those average-priced bottles. Hence the endless dodgy discounts, the grand-sounding, made-up names – Marqués de This and Baron de That – on what are in fact bulk wines made by big agribusiness and just, well, the so-so, soulless sameness of it all.

But be of good heart, for there are glimmers in the dust. The upside of a fixed cost like customs duty is that the more you pay for your wine, the more you get back. If you spend double the average on a bottle then the wine inside it typically accounts for more than half of the purchase price – i.e. *four or five times as much as in our average-priced bottle*. And while there are good wines to be had in the supermarkets at this sweet-spot price level for sure, there are many better bottles to be had elsewhere.

The supermarkets' stranglehold has, in many countries, seen off most of the traditional high-street competition. In the UK, remnants of some of the larger wine chains have been salvaged and are under new (and generally better) ownership, and are worth a look. Mail-order merchants are more of a mixed bag, and a good rule of thumb is that if you see a full-page advertisement in a Sunday supplement or similar, avoid them – you'd be better off if they spent all that money on the wine.

In London, the grand old merchants of St. James's and the City are nothing like as grand as most people assume (and the same goes for their international counterparts). In fact, they are very unstuffy these days and are almost always a pleasure to deal with – as is the case with their equivalents in the shires. You might pay a little over the odds but they have access to all the good stuff at almost every price level.

Most encouragingly of all, as with niche food retail, with microbreweries, farmers' markets and much else besides, a new generation of quality-focused (obsessed, even) small, independent local merchants are springing up all over the place. Use whatever you have at your disposal – the internet, word-of-mouth, stopping people in the street if you have to – to locate yours and don't worry if they're not all *that* local, they'll deliver (on all fronts).

Take advantage of everything they have to offer: ask for their recommendations (at any price level – they will be as proud of their cheapest wines as they are of their best ones) and go to their tastings (free and otherwise); you can learn more about the wines of a particular region in one evening of tasting than by reading a chapter of a book, even this one.

And once you've hunted out a good wine merchant, talk to them about buying wine *en primeur* (when it is offered for sale before being bottled and shipped by the producer). Wine merchants descend *en masse* to the major European wine regions to taste the young wines from the barrel and they have a pretty shrewd idea of how they should turn out. Take their advice on what to buy and then all you have to do is sit back and watch the prices go up once the wine is shipped and then hit the roof when they're ready to drink a few years later. That's the theory. In practice, there is no cheaper way to buy good wine.

THE TOP 5 WINE SHOPPING TIPS

1. *Try to look past the supermarkets.*

2. *Remember that by spending a little more you get a lot more back.*

3. *Check out the offer of wine merchants and high-street wine sellers.*

4. *Hunt down small independents and ask them for specific recommendations.*

5. *Look into buying wine* en primeur.

WHAT TO BUY

Then there is the $64,000 question – what to buy? You don't have to spend that much all at once, of course, and your go-getting independent local merchant will advise you well, but it's always a good idea to buy wines made by people with names and not by corporations. In general, the smaller the number of people involved in making a wine and the smaller the quantity they make of it, the better it will be. Most of us will only put our names to something we're proud of.

Similarly, the best wines are usually made in the most specific of places. That average bottle of wine from South Eastern Australia could be a mix of what Aussie winemakers endearingly call 'juice' from all over an area whose boundary runs for 2000km (the distance from Barcelona to Bucharest) and marks out the bottom-left third of the continent. Meanwhile, regions like the Mornington Peninsula, Heathcote or Coonawarra – although large by European standards – are tiny by comparison and have within them a relatively small number of producers who all know (and compete with) each other. The effect of this in terms of the quality of the wine they produce is spectacular.

The same principle applies throughout most of the infinitely complicated quality regulations in Europe. Small is good, smaller is better and smallest is best. At a basic level, a bottle labelled Côtes du Rhône-Villages – i.e. from a specific group of quality-conscious communes – will almost always be better than a plain old Côtes du Rhône. (In fact, it's a very good idea to join the village people as the same thing applies equally well in Beaujolais and parts of Burgundy, Roussillon and the Loire.)

At the most extreme level in the best wine regions of France, Italy and Germany these demarcation systems zoom in as close as individually named areas of vineyard not much bigger than a football pitch, and even these are often shared among numerous owners. They always produce the most expensive wines, but the key to happiness is to zoom back out a click or two and see how much of the character and quality of the wines of these tiny, overpriced places you can get (and for how little money) in the wider region.

Read the wine writers in newspapers and magazines; while most of them can't write for toffee, they do know what they're talking about and they do want you to drink better wine – even if you're not prepared to spend more money. Ask friends and colleagues about specific wines they enjoy. Most would rather discuss their sex lives or their salaries but the few who are out and proud about their passion for wine will often tell you more than you want to know.

If you're buying blind then it's usually a good idea to avoid labels that feature animals, shouty bright colours and puns or jokey names (in fact, any names other than those of the maker and the place they made it in). If a label looks confident, elegant and understated – in a word, classy – there's a fair chance the wine will be too (though note there are plenty of exceptions to this most inexact of theories).

1. Try to buy wines that people have put their names to, rather than those made by large corporations.

2. Look for wines from as specific a location as possible. Smaller is almost always best.

3. Read wine reviews in newspapers and magazines for steers towards the best bottles out there at all levels.

4. Avoid shouty, bright labels.

5. Steer clear of puns or jokey names (unless you want the joke to be on you).

WINE IN RESTAURANTS

Restaurant wine lists induce in many people something near to terror. The fact that a lot of restaurants make the majority of their profit from the most expensive handful of bottles they sell in a given week doesn't do much to help this. And unless somebody gives us an unlimited expense account, we won't be buying any of them.

Mark-ups are traditionally between 200% and 400% and typically in the middle of that range, but lots of restaurateurs are experimenting with imaginative ways of selling wine; larger selections of wines by-the-glass (sometimes using new inert gas storage systems to avoid their biggest problem – wastage); wine-inclusive menus, which are often good value even if the price looks scary at first; fixed mark-ups (which make more expensive wines a much better deal) and different sizes of carafes priced pro-rata to a full bottle.

A few pointers. Forget you've ever heard of Bordeaux or Burgundy, or Barolo or Barbaresco for that matter – when opting for a glass or bottle of wine in a restaurant it's best and most fun to go off-piste. Yes, you may well come a cropper now and then, but the sommelier will like you and you seldom find bad wine in a good restaurant anyway. Besides, sommeliers are seldom the stern, sneering caricatures of popular imagination – most are young and bursting with enthusiasm to talk about wine. Don't be afraid to tell them how much you want to spend and let them do the rest.

Some people say you should avoid the second-cheapest wine on a list as it's likely to have the highest mark-up. They should talk to my friend for whom buying the second-cheapest wine on a list has become something of an *idée-fixe*. He's very happy with his strategy but they should all get a life – it's as meaningful as taking the cork out of a bottle thinking it well let the wine 'breathe'.

Newly improved regions with a lot of previous to make up for – like Beaujolais, Valpolicella and Chianti – and less-travelled roads like Alsace, the Loire, north-eastern and southern Italy are hot-spots for value. Countries that don't often feature on wine lists – Austria, Portugal, Greece and the rest of south-east Europe – often attract low mark-ups and can be the happiest hunting grounds. You can often check out a restaurant's wine list on its website and plan what to order in advance – but what sort of obsessive lunatic would go to those lengths?

9 STORING AND SERVING RED WINE

SOMETHING LIKE NINETY PER CENT OF WINE IS consumed on the day it is purchased and it strikes me that the amount of tosh talked about the storage of wine may not be unconnected to this fact. And whether we're talking about a *carpe diem* bottle or about one that has been cherished and anticipated for years, the tosh quotient is only exceeded by that which attaches to the serving of it.

The storage question – assuming we are talking about keeping it at home, rather than in a purpose-built facility – is simple: can you find a spot where it is going to improve rather than deteriorate? The serving issue is no biggie either: how can you give the wine you've bought and paid for the best possible chance to shine? With this is mind, the questions to ask about a wine are: Is it the right temperature? Is it likely to improve with some exposure to oxygen? Does it have any sediment? What sort of glasses should it be served in?

STORING WINE

When I first started putting together a little cellar of sorts I used to fret. It was a long way away at my mother's place and a tiny space to contain so much worry. Was it too warm in summer? Too cold in winter? I bought a 'max-min' thermometer – it was a bit of both. Too damp? A tad. Any strong smells? Thankfully not. Too insecure? Probably, but not as insecure as its owner. The wine was always fine – it's a lot less sensitive than it's supposed to be.

I hope it's true that a wine club once gave a dozen members a bottle each from a case of nice claret to store wherever they thought fit until they were ready to drink. The consensus was that the best bottle was the one that had been rolling around in the boot of somebody's car... for five years... in Denmark.

I don't keep any in the car but I do keep most of my wine at home now because a) I'm knocking on a bit and I want to drink it when I choose; and b) because medium-term wines (i.e. for drinking in one to five years) are blissfully happy in a rack in a reasonably cool spot (against a north-facing wall is a good idea) with no direct sunlight. Excessive heat – i.e. anything over 25°C – is the one thing that really is fatal for wine, even for a brief period.

So dig deep, but into your wallet, not the ground and start buying by the case both for wines for immediate drinking and those that won't improve with age (think case discounts and not having to schlep it home) as well as those for 'laying down'. This is a real sweet spot – young wines that cost maybe two or three times the price of the average bottle and that really bloom with a few years of maturation (and at which point they often cost four or five times the average).

The finest wines (which, however you cut it, have to be considered as investments) are best stored with the merchant you buy them from unless you're 100% sure you'll be drinking as opposed to cashing in on them. A quid per bottle per year may sound like a lot of money but the value of these wines increases much more over time if everybody knows exactly where they've been.

1. Cru Bourgeois Bordeaux

2. Southern Rhône, e.g. Vacqueyras and Gigondas

3. Single-village Burgundy

4. Brunello di Montalcino, Vino Nobile di Montepulciano (Italy)

5. Ribera del Duero and Priorat (Spain)

Also, have fun with stashing a few southern hemisphere wines – they don't all improve, but boy, when they do...

SERVING WINE

A lot of peculiar, almost sacramental reverence – can't imagine why – seems to attach itself to the simple subject of serving wine. For the love of God, can't we just ask a few practical questions: Is it cold (or warm) enough? Is there sediment in the bottle? Would it benefit from some air (as almost all wine does)? What about glasses (assuming you're not intending to serve it 'by the neck')?

There may be a cork in the way, of course. A pub-style, counter-mounted extractor would be ideal (but people might *talk*) so maybe somebody could give you a lever-pull (or 'rabbit') model for Christmas? Failing that, a 'double-reach' waiter's friend is best – no space to explain the mechanics here – just trust me.

There's no getting away from the fact that temperature is important in letting any wine put its best foot forward. In fact, it changes everything – put your red in the fridge while you drink the first glass if you don't believe me. Most white wine is drunk too cold and most red too warm. Only light (or crappy) whites should be fridge-cold – it stuns the flavour like a taser – bigger wines need about an hour. All light reds – not just from Beaujolais and the Loire – get a certain pert perkiness from a little kiss of a chill as well. For chilling lots of wine, buy in loads of ice and mix it with water in a bucket – it's much faster.

As for glasses, bigger is better – and always with a turned-in, or tulip, shape to keep in as much aroma as possible. (But they keep in bad smells as well if they're not completely clean, so sniff before you serve – most 'corked' wine is in fact musty glasses). Genuinely corked wine is a rarity but there are numerous other things that can go wrong, from a niggling dishcloth smell in the background to full-on oxidation. Trust your initial instinct and if the first sniff repels rather than attracts then put the cork back in and take the bottle back.

Only fill a third of the way (more room for swirling and sniffing) and then refill often so you don't look like a tight-arse. But do be a tight-arse for picnics and barbies – there's no point serving posh wine outdoors; the loveliness just gets blown away on the breeze. Go for big, bold reds like South American Shiraz and malbecs and old-style Aussies.

See that your butler decants all your wines (whites as well) to get some oxygen on to them and allow the aromas and flavours to open up like blooming flowers. On his day off, just sloosh it out into a jug and then back into the bottle – it's called double-decanting and it makes for minor miracles. Merely taking the cork out in advance is pointless.

As for the feckless, we often pour out a glass and then give the bottle a good shake – assuming there's no sediment. If there is, then pour it out steadily, without stopping, somewhere well-lit where you can see when to stop pouring – i.e. when the kack (or lees) starts to go into the neck – and don't forget to rinse the bottle (or just leave it in the jug). If you cock it up, a pair of tights can be useful (provided they are not being worn at the time).

Wine is in a state of perpetual change – so are wine drinkers. You didn't buy this book because you want to carry on drinking what you're already drinking, so change what you buy, who you buy it from, and how much you spend on it. I don't know anybody who ever did that and regretted it.

THE TOP 5 WINE SERVING TIPS

1. Go big on glass size, with a turned-in shape to keep the aroma in the glass.

2. Only fill a third of a glass at a time.

3. Decant your wine to bring out its flavours and aromas.

4. Pour the wine out slowly and steadily to prevent sediment from escaping.

5. Experiment with light chilling but never serve a red wine fully fridge-cold.

GLOSSARY OF TERMS USED

AGEING While wine is capable of deteriorating with age, complex chemical reactions that take place over time involving the sugars, acids and flavour compounds can improve its colour, aroma and taste. The ability of a wine to age is influenced by numerous factors, including grape variety, vintage, vine-growing practices, wine region and winemaking style.

ASSEMBLAGE A winemaking technique involving the blending of different wines to create a unique and complex product prior to bottling.

BARRIQUE The most common variety of small oak barrel used as containers for the ageing of wine, designed and developed in Bordeaux. A barrique has a capacity of 225 litres (59 gallons).

BIODYNAMIC WINE Wine made using the principles of biodynamic agriculture, a method of organic farming that sees the land, the crops that grow on it and the fauna it supports as part of an ecological whole. The wines are treated with biodynamic preparations applied following phases of the moon and can be unfiltered, which can give them a cloudy appearance.

ÉLEVAGE The process of shaping a wine through techniques such as assemblage, maturation, filtering and fining to transform a raw fermented wine into something resembling its final form.

EN PRIMEUR A method of buying wine before it's bottled and released onto the market, also known as 'wine futures'. Wine purchased in this fashion is often considerably cheaper than it is once it has been bottled and shipped.

FERMENTATION A metabolic process that converts sugar in the grape juice into alcohol and carbon dioxide (a by-product). Red wines are fermented on their skins, which is what gives them their colour.

LAGAR A traditional Spanish or Portugese stone trough in which grapes are trodden in order to extract the juices for fermentation.

MACERATION The winemaking process whereby the tannins, colouring agents and flavour compounds are extracted from the grape skins and seeds. Maceration begins as soon as the grape skins are broken and exposed to heat and continues throughout the fermentation process.

NATURAL WINE Wines made with minimal chemical and technological intervention. These wines are characterized by their low amounts of sulphur, which is often used during the winemaking process as a preservative, the absence of which can lead to wide variations from one bottle of natural wine to another.

OAKING Oak is used in winemaking to vary the flavour, colour, texture and complexity of a wine through the compounds extracted from the wood. It can be introduced in one of two ways: either in the form of a barrel used to store the wine during the fermentation and ageing periods, or as wood chips or staves added to the wine while it ferments in a stainless-steel fermenting vessel.

TANNINS Compounds that exist within the skin, seeds and stems of grapes responsible for making wine taste dry or astringent.

TERROIR The environmental and climatic conditions in which grapes are grown and which give a wine its particular flavour and aroma.

VIGNERON A person who cultivates a vineyard for winemaking.

BIBLIOGRAPHY

A Hedonist in the Cellar: Adventures in Wine, Jay McInerny, Vintage (2007). Most wine writing is good on the wine, not so much on the writing – apparently, being a brilliant novelist is the trick.

Essential Winetasting: The Complete Practical Winetasting Course, Michael Schuster, Mitchell Beazley (revised ed. 2009). In an age obsessed with apparent novelty, cleave to things that last – this will still be good 100 years from now.

Hugh Johnson's Pocket Wine Book 2015, Mitchell Beazley (2014). If there were only ever to be one wine book, this would be it. Annual since 1977, I know of no other book on any subject that encrypts so much into so portable a format (and yet can still amuse).

The Oxford Companion to Wine, ed. Jancis Robinson, 3rd edition, OUP, 2006 (4th edition due Oct 2015). Whatever it is, if it's not in this 800+pp., 4000-entry, million-word masterwork it's not worth knowing. Not exactly portable.

The World Atlas of Wine, ed. Hugh Johnson and Jancis Robinson, Mitchell Beazley (7th edition, 2013). If you can't find it on one of the 200+ maps (which zoom in to locate individual chateaux) in this 400+pp masterwork, it's not worth finding. Text is superb too. Not exactly portable, either.

Windows on the World Complete Wine Course, Kevin Zraly, Sterling, (30th new edition, 2014). The World Trade Center no longer stands but this does.

FILM
Sideways (Alexander Payne, 2004)
Mondovino (Jonathan Nossiter, 2004)
Bottle Shock (Randall Miller, 2008)

ONLINE
wine-pages.com – for UK press wine reviews
erobertparker.com – for detail, lots of detail
wineanorak.com – for interesting stuff
wine-searcher.com – for prices and places
tv.winelibrary.com – discontinued, but still 'out there'

TWITTER
@JancisRobinson
@RandallGrahm
@GaryVee
@EricAsimov
and, er, @GrogansDrinking

TASTING NOTES

Now that you've been persuaded to start something that could in some sense or other be called a 'cellar' you'll want to make some notes. Like children and gardens, a cellar requires patience – and the rewards are similarly satisfying (chief among them being the joy of watching things grow and get better).

NAME/ VINTAGE	DATE PURCHASED	NO. PURCHASED	CONSUMED /OCCASION	COMMENTS

NAME/ VINTAGE	DATE PURCHASED	NO. PURCHASED	CONSUMED /OCCASION	COMMENTS

INDEX

ACKNOWLEDGEMENTS

Ed Griffiths – for getting the ball rolling; Jane O'Shea – for the vision thing; Simon Davis – for turning some words into a book; David Miller – for making it happen; Federica Leonardis – for helping him; Jonathan Ray – for getting me started. And to Leslie, for putting up with it all (again) so gracefully.